Table of Contents

Introduction

Hi there!

So, you're on the ketogenic diet, right? How is it going? Feeling energized, trim and healthy? Great! However, I'm guessing you're really missing those sweet, tasty, gooey, moreish, satisfying desserts. I don't blame you! Dessert has to be one of life's most special treats, and we shouldn't deprive ourselves. I am a true believer that any diet, any nutrition plan, any lifestyle change absolutely *must* include dessert.

I have fantastic news for you...there are SO MANY desserts you can enjoy on the keto diet! Even better? They're all here! (Well, a large collection of them). I have created a collection of entirely keto-friendly desserts which are easy to make and a joy to eat.

We have chocolate, fruity, frozen, hot, dairy-free, cheese-based, baked, and morsel-sized desserts for you to explore. Some desserts are as easy as mixing a few simple ingredients and leaving to set, while others are more complicated and require a longer process (but still super easy!).

Because these recipes are sugar-free and very low carb, you can enjoy them often. However... many use lots of butter and cream so don't go *too* overboard.

I'm so excited for you to explore these recipes and discover some new favorites!

The Keto Diet
What is keto?

The ketogenic diet (as you already know, I am sure) is a diet designed to put the body into a state of ketosis. This is done by *heavily* reducing the number of carbs eaten and increasing the intake of fats. When we eat carbs, our body uses them for energy and stores the excess as glycogen. This means that the fat we eat is stored away as fat (yup, the kinda fat we can see and touch). What's more, when we eat carbs (especially sugars!) our blood sugar spikes. When we *remove* these carbs, our body has to turn to fat as an energy source. When our body starts breaking down fats to use as energy, the liver produces ketones which are also used as energy. And there you have it, a short explanation of the ketosis process.

What you really need to know here (because this book is all about food, after all!) is that the ketogenic diet relies on a specific breakdown of macronutrients (carbs, fats and proteins). The most *crucial* macro to keep an eye on is carbs. The general number most people stick to is 30 grams of net carbs per day. Net carbs is simply the total carbs with the fiber subtracted. You also have to be careful about how much protein you eat too, as too much can actually take you out of ketosis. Many people use this formula for their protein intake while on keto: 0.6 grams of protein per pound of body weight. For example, a 170-pound person would eat 90 grams of protein per day. After a small amount of carbs, the rest of their food intake would be made up of healthy fat.

Many people choose to try the ketogenic to lose weight, especially around the middle. Others try it to increase energy levels, reduce the risk of diabetes or even for fertility purposes. But we will get into the great benefits of the keto diet below!

Interestingly, the ketogenic diet was popular about 100 years ago for the treatment of epilepsy. The ketogenic diet is basically a fancy, calculated way of fasting. Fasting has been used for millennia, as thinkers and holy people fasted as a spiritual practice, but also to boost their energy levels and inspire sharp thinking. That's just a little snippet of history to put the ketogenic diet into context! Fast forward to today, and keto is a popular diet for many people for many reasons, helped along by technology. There are many apps such as MyFitnessPal which calculate the macronutrients in everything you eat, providing you with the correct fat, protein, total carbs, net carbs and calories.

But that's enough of my rambling! Let's get into the benefits of the ketogenic diet...

What are the benefits?

Weight loss

The number one reason why modern people choose to try the ketogenic diet is weight loss. When you eat a high-fat diet, you become satiated and full much sooner than you would with a high-carb or low-fat diet. This helps you to eat smaller portions and therefore fewer calories over time. What's more, by cutting out sugary, starchy foods and replacing them with wholesome, veggie-based foods, you cut out *lots* of calories. The very nature of the ketogenic diet means that the body turns into a fat burning machine, helping to tap into stored fat, leaving you feeling slenderer and leaner! The ketogenic diet also really helps to regulate and boost your insulin sensitivity, which helps with weight loss and vice versa (losing excess weight helps with insulin issues such as insulin resistance!).

Abundant energy and sharper mind

So many keto dieters find that one of the very best side effects is increased energy levels and a sharp mind. The ketones that your body produces while burning fat for energy are actually an awesome source of energy for your brain. This means that your brain works harder, faster and sharper! Get more work done, win any argument and generally feel sharp as a tack.

Disease prevention

The ketogenic diet could help your body to stave off certain diseases such as diabetes, metabolic disease, cancer and even Alzheimer's disease. The ketogenic diet helps to regulate blood sugar levels and weight, both of which are really important factors for health and longevity. By eating lots of healthy fats and nutritious veggies, your heart is also supported! However, it's important to choose healthy fats (avocado, nuts, seeds, cold pressed oils and fish) as opposed to filling yourself with butter, cream and animal fats. By cutting out processed sugars and starchy carbs and replacing them with nutrient-dense plant-based foods and grass-fed meats, your body has a much better chance at functioning at optimal level for decades, with a far lower risk of developing diseases.

Great for the skin

If you approach your keto diet with a healthy mindset and focus on nutrition as well as macros, you'll likely find that your skin becomes clear and glowy. High-fat foods (healthy fats, that is) such as avocados, nuts, seeds, olive oil, flaxseed oil and oily fish are all incredible for the skin. They nourish and hydrate the skin from the inside, leaving you with a healthy, youthful and luminous complexion.

Takes care of blood sugar levels

When you eat sugar and carbs, your blood sugar goes a little wonky. In fact, it spikes and increases. When this happens over and over again, you risk all kinds of complications such as type 2 diabetes and obesity. Out-of-whack blood sugar levels can make you feel sleepy, dizzy and generally not so great. The ketogenic diet can really help to stabilize your blood sugar, helping you to feel energetic and on top of the world. In fact, this is one of the main medical reasons why the ketogenic is recommended!

What can and can't you eat on keto?

The keto-friendly "YES" foods:

These are the low-carb foods which are permitted on the ketogenic diet. Some of them can be eaten liberally, such as leafy greens. Others can be eaten with a little more moderation, such as nuts and berries. Your calorie counter/macro calculator will let you know exactly how many net carbs are in each food, so you will soon learn the right quantities and it will become second nature!

Oils:

- Olive oil
- Avocado oil
- Flaxseed oil
- MCT oil
- Coconut oil
- Walnut oil

Nuts and seeds:

- Almonds
- Walnuts
- Pecans
- Brazil nuts
- Hazelnuts
- Macadamia nuts
- Cashews
- Pumpkin seeds
- Sunflower seeds
- Chia seeds
- Sesame seeds
- Nut and seed butters (plain, no flavors or sugars added)

Low carb veggies:

- Lettuce
- Spinach
- Kale

- Avocado (technically a fruit...but it's an *incredible* keto food, full of healthy fats and fiber)
- Asparagus
- Artichokes
- Cabbage
- Broccoli
- Cauliflower
- Bok choy
- Chard
- Celery
- Green beans
- Mushrooms
- Mustard greens
- Tomatoes
- Zucchini
- Spaghetti squash
- Mung beans
- Cucumber

Berries in moderation:
- All berries are fine, but raspberries and blackberries have fewer carbs than strawberries and blueberries, so keep that in mind. Just stick to a small portion of berries and you'll be fine!

Eggs and soy proteins:
- Free range eggs are a great source of fat and protein without any carbs
- Tofu and tempeh are great protein sources for vegans and vegetarians

Grass-fed meats:
Choose organic, grass-fed meats. As long as there are no seasonings or marinades added, you can enjoy all forms of meat. Ground meat, steaks, roasts, chops, legs... it's all good!
- Bacon
- Beef
- Pork
- Venison
- Lamb

Fish and poultry:
All fish and poultry is 100% permitted as long as it's not pre-seasoned or marinated
Choose free range poultry and wild-caught fish
Salmon is a fantastic choice because it's full of healthy fats and oils

- Salmon
- Tuna
- All white fish
- Chicken
- Turkey

Full fat dairy:

- Full-fat cream
- Full-fat plain, unsweetened yogurt (NO low fat or fat free varieties allowed!)
- Full-fat sour cream
- Full-fat ricotta
- Full-fat mascarpone

Cheese:

- Cheddar
- Brie
- Camembert
- Blue cheese
- Parmesan cheese
- Feta cheese
- Goat cheese
- Colby cheese

Keto sweetener:

- Stevia
- Erythritol
- Xylitol

Herbs and spices:

- All fresh and dried herbs are completely permitted
- Use dried spices to flavor your food, just beware of mixed seasonings and rubs as they can often contain sugar

Keto flours:

- Coconut flour
- Almond flour/ground almonds
- Ground flaxseed
- Ground hazelnuts

Coffee and tea:

- Add cream to your coffee for a fat booster!
- NO sugar in that cup of hot tea! Use a sweetener such as Stevia instead
- NO milk in your tea and coffee, always use cream as milk contains sugar

Alcohol:

- All spirits are okay on keto, in moderation. Note: this does *not* include liqueurs or sugary drinks such as Kahlua or Baileys Irish Cream. Plain, pure spirits such as vodka, gin, whiskey, rum and tequila are all zero-carb as long as you mix them with water, plain soda or zero-carb soda.
- Champagne, dry white wine and red wine are all fine in moderation. For example, one glass of champagne (around 5oz) has a maximum of 2 grams of net carbs.
- Mixers: plain, unflavored soda with fresh citrus is best

Sauces and condiments:

- Full-fat mayonnaise and fresh guacamole are permitted the keto diet as long as they do not contain sugar. Salad dressing made from oil and vinegar is fine, but watch out for store-bought salad dressings which are often packed with sugar.

The keto-banned "NO WAY" foods:

Pasta, noodles, bread and rice:

- All pasta, noodles, bread and rice are off limits. Basically, anything made from flour or grains is out of bounds.

Beans, lentils, chickpeas:

- Unfortunately, beans, lentils and chickpeas are all prohibited on the keto diet because of their high carb content. These foods are in the legume food group and are all banned on keto. This also includes peas and peanuts.

Baked goods:

- Traditional baked goods such as cakes, cookies, bars, breads, scones and cupcakes are all out of the question on keto. If they contain flour and sugar, get rid of them.

Sugary treats:

- Candy, chocolate (except 72% cocoa dark chocolate), ice cream and all things in the candy aisle are not allowed on keto. If you're craving a sweet treat, pick a recipe from this book!

Juice, soda, premixed alcoholic drinks:

- Fruit juices, sodas and premixed alcoholic drinks ("alcopops") are filled with sugar and are not ketogenic-approved. Stick to water, plain soda water, tea and coffee.

Grains:

- Grains such as rice, quinoa, oats and barley are all ruled out on keto because they are high-carb foods. You can use cauliflower and broccoli as rice substitutes.

Milk:

- Milk contains sugar and is therefore not permitted on keto. Stick to full-fat cream or unsweetened nut milks such as almond milk.

Most fruits:

- The only fruits you can eat on keto are avocados and berries (in moderation). Avoid all other fruits, especially bananas. Fruits are high-carb, high-sugar foods. While fruits are not unhealthy, they're simply too carb-rich and therefore negate the ketogenic process.

Starchy veggies:
- Starchy veggies such as potato, sweet potato, corn, yams, peas, carrots and beets are not keto-friendly as they are high in carbs. Stick to leafy greens and low-carb veggies as listed above.

Sauces and condiments:
- Stay away from store-bought sauces, condiments and marinades as they are often packed with sugars. Make your own dressings, sauces and marinades at home so you know exactly what's in them.

Tips for choosing the right keto foods
- Check the labels on any packaged foods. Does it contain sugar? Put it back! Does it have a high net carb count? Put it back!
- Try to choose foods which are close to the source and haven't been processed or packaged. Think meat, eggs, nuts/seeds, veggies, full-fat diary, oils etc.
- Install a calorie-counter app on your phone so you can always check the macros of any food if you're unsure
- Does it contain flour, sugar or starchy veggies? No go!
- Keep an eye on your portion sizes. If one portion is perfectly balanced with the right amount of carbs, an extra portion may tip you over the edge. If you're still hungry after dinner? Fill up on a fresh salad with an olive oil dressing

Can you really eat dessert on keto?

Uh, YES! Of course. Keto isn't about cutting out certain meals or recipes...it's about sticking to the correct macros. This means that as long as your dessert is within the parameters of your macros, it's completely permitted! Luckily for us, ingredients such as butter, cream, sour cream, mascarpone, cream cheese and eggs are all wonderfully keto-friendly foods...and perfect dessert ingredients too.

When it comes to sugar, there are many non-sugar sweeteners out there which are 100% keto approved. Stevia, erythritol and xylitol are the most popular sweeteners as they don't spike the blood sugar at all. I think that Stevia is the best sweetener as you only need a very small amount and it contains barely any carbs or calories.

Note: these recipes were all formulated using STEVIA which is extremely sweet and only requires 1 tsp per 1 cup of regular sugar. Other sweeteners are less sweet and require a far larger measure. My advice is to use Stevia for these recipes to get the best result.

Concerned about the issue of flour? No worries! We use ground almonds and sometimes ground hazelnuts. Ground almonds provide awesome fat and protein, with more fiber than regular flour. Ground almonds do give a denser result, but to me, that's a great thing! A dense, fudgy cake is nothing to be mad about.

Keto dessert ingredient staples (staples in these recipes, at least!)

- Heavy cream
- *Real* butter (grass-fed butter, *no* margarine or butter substitutes please!)
- Coconut oil, canola oil, olive oil, flaxseed oil
- Cocoa powder (unsweetened, always)
- Pure vanilla extract (no essence or imitations)
- Fresh mint
- Flavor essences (such as almond or caramel)
- Cream cheese (plain, full fat)
- Espresso powder
- Mascarpone cheese (plain, full fat)
- Keto sweeteners such as Stevia
- Almonds, hazelnuts and walnuts (ground and whole)
- Salt (for bringing out chocolate flavor)
- Eggs (always free range)
- Berries (frozen, fresh and freeze-dried)
- Lemon zest and juice
- 72% cocoa dark chocolate (a small amount, and it *must* be at least 72% cocoa!)

Keto Desserts

About these recipes

Serves

Each recipe will have a "Serves" indication at the start. This tells you how many servings the recipe will yield. It's important to note that the nutritional value per serving has been calculated according to this number. If you find that the recipe yields more or fewer servings than indicated, you can shuffle the nutritional value to get a more accurate reading. For example, if the recipe states that it yields 4 servings and the calorie count per serving is 250, just multiply the calories (250) with the servings (4). You then get the calorie count for the entire recipe (1000). If you find that the recipe yields 3 servings for your needs, just divide 1000 by 3 to get the accurate nutritional value.

Time

Each recipe has a "Time" indication at the start which tells you approximately how long the recipe takes to make from start to finish. Some recipes require chilling time in the fridge and this is indicated in the "Time" provided. You may be a very fast cook or a leisurely one, so take that into account when planning your dessert making sessions.

Ingredients

- *Vanilla:* only use pure vanilla *extract,* not vanilla *essence.* Vanilla extract has been taken from real vanilla pods, while essence is simply a chemical concoction made to resemble vanilla. You could also use vanilla pods if you're super fancy (scrape out the seeds inside and use those instead of extract).
- *Chocolate:* yes, chocolate is allowed on keto! In fact, there's an entire *section* dedicated to it in this very book. However, you must only buy 72% (at least) cocoa dark chocolate. Don't go for milk, white or "slightly" dark chocolate. 72% cocoa dark chocolate has less sugar and more rich, chocolatey goodness.
- *Cocoa:* always use high-quality, unsweetened cocoa powder.
- *Butter:* you 100% must use real butter. Margarine or butter alternatives are not allowed! Butter gives a far, *far* better flavor and is actually better for you than margarine.
- *Cream:* ah, delicious cream. Always buy full-fat, whole, heavy cream. Don't be tempted by milk or half and half.
- *Ground almonds:* ground almonds can be a little expensive but it's really worth it for the sake of high-quality keto desserts. Make sure you purchase pure ground almonds with no added sweeteners. The ingredients list should feature nothing but almonds! Oh, and a helpful tip for storage: store your ground almonds in the fridge so they don't become rancid or fall prey to weevils or pantry moths.

- *Sea salt:* sea salt appears in many of these recipes. I love the mild saltiness and the flaky texture. Maldon Sea Salt is my chosen brand!
- *Eggs:* always buy free-range eggs! They're more nutritious and come from ethical sources.
- *Sweeteners:* NOTE that these recipes were made with Stevia as the preferred keto-friendly sweetener. You can use another sweetener if you like, but it just means that you may have to adjust the quantities and take your macros into account. Be aware that stevia is sweeter than other keto sweeteners, so ALWAYS taste the batter to test the sweetness. You may like a sweeter dessert or a milder dessert, so it's really important to use your taste buds and adjust the sweetener quantities as needed.

Method

Each recipe is broken down into a numbered process which is easy to follow and covers every step of the way. While these recipes are super simple and easy to make, there are a few pointers I'd like to chat about before we begin, just to ensure you get the very best result possible.

- *Melting chocolate:* many of the chocolate-based and custard-based recipes require a bowl and saucepan to melt the chocolate and butter. This is super easy, and I find it safer than using the microwave which can burn chocolate and over-heat butter. You just need a heatproof bowl (such as a Pyrex glass bowl) and a saucepan. The bowl should sit over the water in the saucepan and not *in the water*. The water should not touch the bottom of the bowl as you risk burning the ingredients that way. This method allows you to continuously stir the mixture and keep a constant eye on it so it doesn't burn, curdle or over-thicken.
- *Baking and ovens:* all ovens are different. Some are very hot and some run a little cooler. My oven may bake a cake in 30 minutes while yours may bake it in 25! For this reason, always take the baking times as an approximate suggestion. Let's say the recipe states to bake the cake/recipe for 25 minutes, start checking on it at around 18 minutes just to be sure. An overcooked, dry baked good cannot be reversed, but an under-baked dish can be put back in the oven!
- *Whipping cream:* many recipes require you to whip cream. While this is the easiest thing to do...it can be overdone, and that's no good! Stop whipping your cream when it reaches that soft, pillowy stage. If you keep going, you may reach that buttery, overly-thick stage which just isn't so pleasant. We want our whipped cream to be soft like a cloud, not thick like a sponge!
- *Chilling:* many recipes require you to pop the finished result into the fridge or freezer for a period of time. I find that it's always best to simply make the dessert the night before it is required. That way, there's always ample time for the dish to

set and freeze. You can always leave it out at room temperature for a wee while to soften, but you can't speed up the chilling process.

Nutritional information

Each recipe has a nutritional table which lets you know exactly how many calories, fats, proteins, total carbs and net carbs each serving contains. "Net carbs" is the total carbs with the fiber subtracted. If a recipe has a really high "Total carb" count and a much lower "Net carb" count, you know that it's packed with lots of fiber. As these are dessert recipes, don't be too alarmed if you come across a few which have super high calorie counts...butter and creamy ingredients sure do add up!

Chocolate Desserts

Of course we are starting the recipe section with a big, rich, gooey, chocolatey bang! We cannot eat milk or white chocolate, but we can eat 72% cocoa dark chocolate and cocoa powder, obviously. In fact, cocoa powder is a wonderful source of antioxidants, so really, these desserts are complete health foods (let's just pretend). I am delighted to present you with mousse, brownies, ice cream, fudge sauce, cupcakes, chocolate pie and more...

Chocolate Mousse

Airy, rich, decadent chocolate mousse is always a pleaser. Serve it for a cooling Summer dessert at a dinner party, or whip up a batch with the kids for a healthy-ish treat which won't give them a sugar high and won't kick you out of ketosis. The crazy thing about this dessert is that it's really just a fancy whipped cream which mimics a traditional mousse spectacularly. This is great because it means there are no raw eggs and very little effort required.

Serves: 4

Time: approximately 10 minutes plus 2 hours chilling time in the fridge

Ingredients:

- 1 cup heavy whipping cream (1 cup *before* whipping)
- 3 Tbsp unsweetened cocoa powder
- 1 tsp vanilla extract (pure, no sugar added)
- 1 tsp Stevia/your preferred keto sweetener
- Pinch of salt

Method:

1. Place all ingredients into a large bowl and use an electric egg beater to whip everything together until the cream is soft but not stiff
2. Taste the mousse and assess the sweetness, add more sweetener if you prefer a sweeter mousse
3. Spoon the mousse into glass dessert cups and pop into the fridge to chill for at least 2 hours
4. Serve with a dusting of cocoa powder over top!

Nutritional Information:

- **Calories:** 227
- **Fat:** 22.5 grams
- **Protein:** 1.9 grams
- **Total carbs:** 4.9 grams
- **Net carbs:** 3.4 grams

Mint-Choc Chip Whip

Here we have another easy whipped cream dessert! This time, we are celebrating one of the very best flavor combinations ever...mint and chocolate. Instead of going through the process of making ice cream, we are skipping the middleman and simply going straight for the cream. I use a drop of green food coloring for fun, but you can leave it out if you prefer!

Serves: 5

Time: approximately 10 minutes plus 2 hours chilling time in the fridge

Ingredients:

- 1 cup heavy whipping cream (1 cup *before* whipping)
- 1 tsp Stevia/your preferred keto sweetener
- Pinch of salt
- 1 or 2 drops of green food coloring (optional)
- ½ cup fresh mint leaves, finely chopped
- Few drops of peppermint essence (optional, but it gives a more minty flavor)
- 1 ½ oz 72% cocoa dark chocolate chips

Method:

1. Place the cream, sweetener, salt, food coloring, mint and peppermint extract into a large bowl and use an electric egg beater to whip until the cream is thick and soft
2. Fold the chocolate chips into the cream mixture
3. Spoon the mixture into five dessert dishes and place into the fridge to chill for at least 2 hours
4. Serve with a fresh mint leaf!

Nutritional Information:

- **Calories:** 213
- **Fat:** 20.2 grams
- **Protein:** 1.5 grams
- **Total carbs:** 6.3 grams
- **Net carbs:** 5.5 grams

Gooey Chocolate Brownies

I bet you were waiting for the chocolate brownie recipe! Well, here it is, and it's fantastic. This brownie is super rich, gooey and keto friendly. Make sure to use high-quality 72% cocoa dark chocolate and free range eggs. Best served warm, with a dollop of whipped cream.

Serves: 16

Time: approximately 40 minutes

Ingredients:

- 5 oz 72% cocoa dark chocolate
- 5 oz butter
- 3 eggs
- 2 tsp vanilla extract (pure, unsweetened)
- 1 cup ground almonds
- 3 Tbsp unsweetened cocoa powder
- 1 tsp Stevia/your preferred keto sweetener
- 1 heaping tsp sea salt

Method:

1. Preheat the oven to 360 degrees Fahrenheit and line a brownie pan with baking paper
2. Place the chocolate and butter into a heatproof bowl and place over a pot of simmering water. Stir as the butter and chocolate melt together. Remove from the heat and set aside to cool
3. Add the eggs and vanilla to the melted chocolate and butter mixture and whisk until thoroughly combined
4. Stir the ground almonds, cocoa, sweetener and salt into the chocolate mixture until smooth and combined
5. Spread the batter into your prepared pan and place into the oven to bake for about 20-30 minutes depending on your oven and your preferred doneness. I like my brownies to be gooey so I only cooked mine for 20 minutes!
6. Leave to cool slightly before cutting into squares and serving
7. Freeze any leftovers and have them on hand for your next chocolate craving

Nutritional Information:

- **Calories:** 148
- **Fat:** 12.9 grams
- **Protein:** 3.3 grams
- **Total carbs:** 7.3 grams
- **Net carbs:** 4.9 grams

Fudgy R18 Sauce

We all need a special chocolate sauce recipe in our back pocket to whip out whenever we need to dress ice cream, cake, mousse or even strawberries. This sauce is keto-friendly and has a delectable hit of rum...I won't tell if you won't!

Serves: 5
Time: 20 minutes
Ingredients:

- 4 oz 72% cocoa dark chocolate
- 1 cup heavy cream
- 2 Tbsp cocoa powder
- ½ tsp Stevia/your preferred keto sweetener
- 3 Tbsp dark rum
- Pinch of sea salt

Method:

1. Place the chocolate and cream into a heatproof bowl over a saucepan of water and stir as the chocolate melts into the cream
2. Take the bowl off the heat and whisk the cocoa powder, stevia, rum and salt into the mixture until smooth and silky
3. Give it a taste...add more rum, salt and sweetener to suit your taste preferences!
4. Pour into a pouring jug and store in the fridge until required

Nutritional Information:

- **Calories:** 313
- **Fat:** 28 grams
- **Protein:** 3 grams
- **Total carbs:** 10 grams
- **Net carbs:** 6 grams

Chocolate and Raspberry Cupcakes

Chocolate and raspberry make a beautiful pair, especially when they're paired in the form of a soft, tasty cupcake. We use ground almonds instead of flour, of course. Make sure not to overbake these, as there's nothing more disappointing than a dry cupcake!

Serves: 12

Time: approximately 30 minutes

Ingredients:

- 4 oz butter
- 3 oz 72% cocoa dark chocolate
- 6 eggs
- 2 tsp vanilla extract
- 3 Tbsp cocoa powder
- 1 ½ tsp Stevia/your preferred keto sweetener
- 1 cup ground almonds
- 1 tsp baking powder
- Pinch of salt
- ½ cup heavy cream
- 1 cup raspberries

Cream frosting:

- 1 cup heavy whipping cream
- 2 Tbsp cocoa powder
- 1 tsp Stevia/your preferred keto sweetener

Method:

1. Preheat the oven to 360 degrees Fahrenheit and line a 12-hole muffin pan with cupcake cases
2. Place the butter and chocolate into a heatproof bowl and place over a saucepan of boiling water. Stir until the butter and chocolate have melted together
3. Remove the bowl from the heat and leave to cool for about 5 minutes
4. Add the eggs and vanilla to the cooled chocolate mixture and whisk until thoroughly combined and smooth
5. Sift the cocoa powder, stevia, ground almonds and salt into the chocolate mixture and fold them in until the ingredients are just combined, but don't overmix
6. Fold the cream and raspberries into the batter
7. Spoon the batter into the cupcake cases
8. Place the tray into the preheated oven and bake for about 20 minutes or until the cakes are just set but still a little gooey in the middle
9. Leave the cupcakes to cool completely

10. To create the cream frosting: use a whisk or electric egg beaters to whip the cream, cocoa powder and stevia together until fluffy and soft
11. Pipe or spoon the cream frosting over the cupcakes before serving

Nutritional Information:

- **Calories:** 306
- **Fat:** 29 grams
- **Protein:** 7 grams
- **Total carbs:** 8 grams
- **Net carbs:** 4 grams

Chocolate Self-Saucing Pudding

Chocolate self-saucing pudding was one of the very first desserts I ever learnt to make on my own. It's a really magical dessert because it creates its own delicious sauce simply by adding hot water over top of the batter before baking. Serve with whipped cream and you'll be in keto chocolate heaven.

Serves: 6
Time: approximately 50 minutes
Ingredients:

- 4 oz butter, melted
- ½ cup heavy cream
- 2 eggs, lightly beaten
- 1 cup ground almonds
- 3 Tbsp cocoa powder
- 1 ½ tsp Stevia/your preferred keto sweetener
- 1 tsp baking powder
- 1 tsp sea salt

Sauce:

- 1 cup boiling water
- 3 Tbsp cocoa powder
- 3 tsp Stevia/your preferred keto sweetener

Method:

1. Preheat the oven to 360 degrees Fahrenheit and grease a brownie pan or any rectangular baking dish with butter
2. Whisk together the melted butter, cream and eggs until combined
3. Sift the ground almonds, cocoa powder, sweetener, baking powder and salt into the wet ingredients and stir until combined
4. Spoon the batter into your prepared dish
5. Combine the cocoa powder and sweetener in a small cup and sprinkle over the batter
6. Pour the boiling water over the batter (carefully!)
7. Carefully place the dish into the oven and bake for about 25-30 minutes or until just cooked but still saucy and gooey
8. Serve hot or warm, with cream!

Nutritional Information:

- **Calories:** 332
- **Fat:** 33 grams
- **Protein:** 7 grams
- **Total carbs:** 9 grams
- **Net carbs:** 5 grams

Flourless Chocolate Cake

Flourless chocolate cake is dense, fudgy and very rich. It's flatter than a regular chocolate cake, but that's okay! It's a wonderful recipe to use for dinner parties or a special guest. Serve with a generous dollop of whipped cream or a scoop of keto vanilla ice cream.

Serves: 12

Time: approximately

Ingredients:

- 8 oz 72% cocoa dark chocolate
- 7 oz butter
- 2 tsp vanilla extract
- 2 Tbsp espresso powder dissolved in 2 Tbsp hot water
- 1 ½ tsp Stevia/your preferred keto sweetener
- 1 ¾ cups ground almonds
- 6 eggs, yolks and whites separated

Method:

1. Preheat the oven to 350 degrees Fahrenheit and line a cake pan with baking paper
2. Place the chocolate and butter into a heatproof bowl and place over a saucepan of boiling water. Stir as the butter and chocolate melt together, remove from the heat
3. Stir the vanilla, espresso and sweetener into the chocolate mixture
4. Whisk the egg yolks and ground almonds into the chocolate mixture until thoroughly combined and smooth
5. Use an electric beater to beat the egg whites until stiff (lift the beaters up and there should be stiff peaks of egg white standing up without flopping over)
6. Very carefully and gently fold the egg whites into the chocolate batter, careful not to knock the air out of the egg whites!
7. Spoon the batter into your prepared pan and place into the oven to bake for about 35-40 minutes or until just set but still a little soft in the middle
8. Leave the cake to cool before turning out, slicing and serving with cream or ice cream

Nutritional Information:

- **Calories:** 344
- **Fat:** 31 grams
- **Protein:** 8 grams
- **Total carbs:** 9 grams
- **Net carbs:** 4 grams

Chocolate Hazelnut Tart

What chocolate lover doesn't like chocolate and hazelnut?! It's possibly the most luxurious flavor combination ever. This recipe combines chocolate and hazelnuts in the form of an elegant, nutty, delicate-yet-rich tart. It's best served with a dollop of whipped cream or sweetened mascarpone.

Serves: 12

Time: approximately 45 minutes

Ingredients:

- 1 cup ground hazelnuts
- ⅓ cup ground almonds
- 5 oz butter, melted
- 1 tsp Stevia/your preferred keto sweetener
- 7 oz 72% cocoa dark chocolate
- 3 oz butter
- 4 egg yolks
- ¾ cup heavy cream
- 1 tsp hazelnut essence (optional)
- 2 tsp Stevia/your preferred keto sweetener
- 1 tsp sea salt
- Sea salt to sprinkle over top (optional)

Method:

1. Preheat the oven to 360 degrees Fahrenheit and thoroughly grease a pie dish with butter
2. Combine the ground hazelnuts, ground almonds, melted butter and the first measure of sweetener until you have a sandy-textured mixture
3. Press the nut mixture into your prepared pie dish and try your best to press the mixture up the sides
4. Pop the pie dish into the oven to allow the nutty base to bake for 10 minutes
5. Make the filling: place the chocolate and butter into a heatproof bowl and place over a saucepan of boiling water. Stir as the chocolate and butter melt together. Remove from the heat and leave to cool
6. Whisk the egg yolks, cream, hazelnut essence, sweetener and sea salt into the chocolate mixture until super smooth
7. Pour the filling into the prebaked pie crust and place back into the oven to bake for about 15 minutes or until the filling is just set but still a little wobbly in the center
8. Leave the pie to cool before serving
9. Optional: sprinkle the pie with a little pinch of sea salt before serving

Nutritional Information:

- **Calories:** 400
- **Fat:** 39 grams
- **Protein:** 6 grams
- **Total carbs:** 9 grams
- **Net carbs:** 4 grams

Chocolate Chili Pie

Here we have another chocolate dessert in pie form! This pie is spiked with the heat of chili for a unique and totally sophisticated result. The base is a buttery concoction made from ground almonds, butter, salt and cocoa powder. The pie is topped with pillowy whipped cream to balance the sharpness of the chili and sweetness of the chocolate...not that sweetness is a bad thing around these parts! Note: yes, there is cornstarch in this recipe but only a wee bit so don't worry! It won't tip your carb scale at all.

Serves: 10

Time: approximately 40 minutes

Ingredients:

- 1 cup ground almonds
- 3 ½ oz butter, melted
- 2 Tbsp cocoa powder
- Pinch of salt
- 2 tsp Stevia/your preferred keto sweetener
- 2 Tbsp cornstarch
- 2 ½ cups heavy cream
- 7 oz 72% cocoa dark chocolate
- 4 egg yolks in a small bowl
- 2 tsp vanilla extract
- 1 tsp chili powder
- 1 cup heavy cream
- 1 Tbsp cocoa powder
- ½ tsp Stevia/your preferred keto sweetener

Method:

1. Preheat the oven to 360 degrees Fahrenheit and grease a pie dish with butter
2. Combine the ground almonds, melted butter, cocoa powder and salt
3. Press the almond mixture into your prepared dish (up the sides is best, but don't worry if it's a bit messy and crumbly). Place the dish into your preheated oven to bake for 10 minutes
4. Combine the cornstarch and sweetener with 2 Tbsp of the cream measure to create a slurry (just take the cream out of the 2 ½ cups) and set aside
5. Place the chocolate and remaining cream into a heatproof bowl and place over a saucepan of boiling water and stir as it melts together until smooth
6. Place a small splash of the chocolate/cream mixture into the bowl of egg yolks and whisk to combine thoroughly

7. Transfer the egg yolk mixture into the bowl of chocolate/cream mixture (it should still be over the saucepan of boiling water) and whisk thoroughly

8. Add the vanilla, chili and cornstarch mixture into the bowl and keep whisking as it thickens to a custard-like consistency

9. Pour the custard into your prebaked pie crust and smooth out the top

10. Place the pie into the fridge to set and cool for at least five hours or overnight

11. Make the cream topping just before serving: beat the cream, cocoa and sweetener until soft and thick. Spread over the pie just before serving!

Nutritional Information:

- **Calories:** 247
- **Fat:** 21 grams
- **Protein:** 4 grams
- **Total carbs:** 9 grams
- **Net carbs:** 5 grams

Mocha Cake

Coffee and chocolate...my two biggest vices...it would be stupid not to put them together in a cake! This cake has a mocha frosting and a perfect mix of chocolate and coffee flavor. And hey, both cocoa and coffee are fantastic sources of antioxidants! This cake is basically health food...(wink wink).

Serves: 12
Time: approximately 45 minutes
Ingredients:

- 7 oz butter, softened
- 2 tsp Stevia/your preferred keto sweetener
- 4 eggs
- 2 tsp vanilla extract
- 2 Tbsp instant espresso powder, dissolved in 1 Tbsp water
- 2 Tbsp cocoa powder
- 1 ½ cups ground almonds
- 2 tsp baking powder
- Pinch of salt

Frosting:

- 8 oz full-fat plain cream cheese
- 4 oz butter, softened
- 3 tsp Stevia/your preferred keto sweetener
- 2 tsp espresso powder, dissolved in 2 tsp hot water

Method:

1. Preheat the oven to 360 degrees Fahrenheit and line a cake pan with baking paper
2. Beat the butter, sweetener, eggs and vanilla extract with electric beaters until soft, creamy and fluffy
3. Add the coffee mixture, cocoa powder, ground almonds, baking powder and salt, stir until just combined
4. Pour the batter into your prepared cake pan and bake in your preheated oven for about 30-35 minutes or until a skewer comes out clean
5. Leave the cake to cool completely
6. Make the frosting: using an electric egg beater, beat together the cream cheese and butter until combined and creamy. Add the stevia and espresso mixture and beat until thoroughly combined
7. Spread the frosting over the cooled cake
8. Slice and serve with a cup of hot coffee!

Nutritional Information:

- **Calories:** 464
- **Fat:** 45 grams
- **Protein:** 10 grams
- **Total carbs:** 9 grams
- **Net carbs:** 5 grams

Salted Chocolate and Chili Sauce

We absolutely needed another chocolate sauce recipe in this section, because one is just not enough. This recipe includes salt and chili, both of which are fantastic partners for chocolate. They add a savory flavor and a hit of heat, creating a unique and grown-up flavor profile.

Serves: 6
Time: approximately 15 minutes
Ingredients:

- 5 oz 72% cocoa dark chocolate
- 1 ½ cups heavy cream
- ½ tsp sea salt
- ½ tsp chili powder
- 1 tsp Stevia/your preferred keto sweetener

Method:

1. Place the chocolate and cream into a heatproof bowl and place over a saucepan of boiling water. Stir as the chocolate and cream melt together
2. Add the sea salt, chili and sweetener to the chocolate mixture and stir to combine
3. Transfer the sauce into a pouring jug and keep in the fridge until needed
4. When it's time to use the sauce, heat it up in the microwave to get it back to pouring consistency
5. Serve over keto ice cream, brownies or cake!

Nutritional Information:

- **Calories:** 344
- **Fat:** 32 grams
- **Protein:** 3 grams
- **Total carbs:** 9 grams
- **Net carbs:** 5 grams

Chocolate and Strawberry Ice Cream Bars

Technically, this recipe could also belong the frozen section or the fruity section...but I think that chocolate is the key ingredient so its rightful place is in the chocolate section! This recipe uses avocado for a thick, smooth, creamy texture.

For this recipe you will need a popsicle mold. They're super cheap and sold in most department stores or cookware stores. There are more popsicle-inspired recipes to come, so it's worth buying a mold or two.

Serves: 10

Time: approximately 10 minutes to prep plus overnight to freeze

Ingredients:

- 2 avocados, flesh scooped out
- 2 cups heavy cream
- 3 Tbsp cocoa powder
- 1 tsp Stevia/your preferred keto sweetener
- 1 cup chopped fresh strawberries

Method:

1. Place the avocado flesh in a food processor and blitz until super smooth and creamy
2. With an electric egg beater, whip the cream, cocoa powder and stevia until thick, soft and fluffy
3. Fold the smooth avocado into the cream mixture then fold the strawberries through
4. Spoon the mixture into your popsicle molds, put the lids on and place into the freezer overnight
5. Leave the bars in the molds at room temperature for a few minutes before sliding them out and enjoying in the sun!

Nutritional Information:

- **Calories:** 220
- **Fat:** 22 grams
- **Protein:** 2 grams
- **Total carbs:** 6 grams
- **Net carbs:** 3 grams

Fruity/Berry Desserts

Most fruits aren't keto-friendly. However, we can get creative with modest portions of berries, citrus zests and natural essences. I can't resist a citrus dessert, so I have created a lemon tart (the classic!) and lemon curd. I also have a true soft spot for berry desserts so we have berry crumbles, cupcakes, pies and icy coulis. There's also a cheeky rhubarb recipe thrown in there too! These recipes are fantastic for your keto friends who aren't really into chocolate (strange people, but to each their own!)

Lemon Tart

We are starting with one of the most classic, delicious desserts of all: lemon tart. A lemon tart should be smooth, creamy and very lemony indeed. Personally, I love a very tangy lemon tart! Serve with whipped cream to balance out the sharpness of the lemon.

Serves: 8

Time: approximately 40 minutes

Ingredients:

- 1 ½ cups ground almonds
- 3 ½ oz butter, melted
- Zest of 1 lemon
- 5 eggs
- 1 cup heavy cream
- ½ cup fresh lemon juice
- 1 ½ tsp Stevia/your preferred keto sweetener

Method:

1. Preheat the oven to 360 degrees Fahrenheit and thoroughly grease a pie dish with butter
2. Combine the ground almonds, butter and lemon zest. Press the almond mixture into your prepared pie dish. Pop the dish into the oven to bake for 10 minutes
3. Place the eggs, cream, lemon juice and sweetener into a food processor and blitz until combined and smooth
4. Pour the creamy mixture into your prebaked pie crust
5. Place the pie (very carefully!) into the oven and bake for about 20 minutes or until the filling is set but still very slightly wobbly in the center
6. Leave to cool before serving with a dollop of whipped cream!

Nutritional Information:

- **Calories:** 345
- **Fat:** 33 grams
- **Protein:** 9 grams
- **Total carbs:** 8 grams
- **Net carbs:** 5 grams

Raspberry Crumble

Picture it: a fruity crumble...hot from the oven...with a very generous pour of heavy cream...heavenly, right? This crumble features raspberries as the fruit base, with a buttery, cinnamon-spiked crumble on top.

Serves: 5
Time: approximately 35 minutes
Ingredients:

- 2 cups raspberries (fresh or frozen)
- 1 cup ground almonds
- ½ cup dried unsweetened coconut
- 4 oz butter, cold
- 2 tsp Stevia/your preferred keto sweetener
- Pinch of salt
- 1 tsp ground cinnamon
- ½ cup slivered almonds

Method:

1. Preheat the oven to 360 degrees Fahrenheit and have a small baking dish waiting by
2. Place the raspberries into the bottom of the dish and set aside
3. Place the ground almonds, coconut, butter, stevia, salt and cinnamon into a food processor and pulse until it resembles a crumbly, sandy texture with a few larger butter chunks (pea-sized)
4. Sprinkle the crumble over the raspberries
5. Sprinkle the slivered almonds over the crumble
6. Place the crumble into the oven and bake for about 25 minutes or until the crumble is nice and golden!
7. Serve with plenty of heavy cream

Nutritional Information:

- **Calories:** 395
- **Fat:** 37 grams
- **Protein:** 7 grams
- **Total carbs:** 14 grams
- **Net carbs:** 6 grams

Strawberry shortcakes

The cutest dessert ever! Strawberry shortcakes are dainty, tasty, pretty and completely perfect for afternoon tea parties or simply a yummy sweet treat any time. We slice the cakes in half and fill them with sliced strawberries and whipped cream...mmm, dreamy.

Serves: 12

Time: approximately 35 minutes

Ingredients:

- 3 cups ground almonds
- 1 ½ tsp Stevia/your preferred keto sweetener
- Pinch of salt
- 1 tsp baking powder
- 3 eggs
- 1 cup heavy cream
- 2 tsp vanilla extract
- Few drops of pink food coloring (optional)
- 1 cup sliced fresh strawberries
- 1 cup heavy cream
- 2 tsp Stevia/your preferred keto sweetener

Method:

1. Preheat the oven to 360 degrees Fahrenheit and line a 12-hole muffin pan with cupcake cases
2. In a large bowl, combine the ground almonds, sweetener, salt and baking powder
3. In a small bowl, whisk together the eggs, cream, vanilla and food coloring
4. Pour the wet ingredients into the dry ingredients and stir until just combined
5. Spoon the batter into your prepared cupcake cases and pop the tray into the oven to bake for about 25 minutes or until the cakes are just set and a skewer comes out clean
6. Leave the cakes to cool completely
7. Whip the cream and stevia until the cream is soft and fluffy
8. Slice the cupcakes in half (so you have a top and bottom) and place a layer of strawberry slices onto the bottom half. Place a dollop of cream on top of the strawberries and place the top half of the cupcake on top of the cream
9. Serve right away so the cream stays fresh and fluffy!

Nutritional Information:

- **Calories:** 301
- **Fat:** 28 grams
- **Protein:** 7 grams
- **Total carbs:** 8 grams
- **Net carbs:** 5 grams

Blueberry mascarpone pie

Blueberry pie, an antioxidant-filled classic. Instead of a pie lid, we slather it with sweetened mascarpone cheese. Mascarpone is deliciously thick, rich and creamy and goes so well with blueberries. A fantastic "keto-fied" version of a fan favorite! The net carb count for this recipe is a little higher than others, so pair it with a really low carb dinner and you're good to go!

Serves: 10

Time: approximately 35 minutes

Ingredients:

- 1 ½ cups ground almonds
- 4 oz butter, melted
- 1 egg, lightly beaten
- 1 tsp Stevia/your preferred keto sweetener
- Pinch of salt
- 3 cups blueberries (fresh or frozen)
- ½ tsp ground cinnamon
- 9 oz full-fat mascarpone cheese
- 1 tsp Stevia/your preferred keto sweetener
- 2 tsp vanilla extract

Method:

1. Preheat the oven to 360 degrees Fahrenheit and grease a pie dish with butter
2. Combine the ground almonds, butter, egg, stevia and salt until thoroughly combined
3. Press the almond mixture into your prepared pie dish and place into the preheated oven to bake for 12 minutes
4. Place the blueberries into the prebaked pie crust and sprinkle the berries with cinnamon
5. Place the pie back into the oven and bake for about 10 minutes or until the blueberries are soft and juicy
6. With a fork, gently press the cooked blueberries to create a mushier, softer texture, leave to cool
7. Combine the mascarpone, sweetener and vanilla together until smooth and creamy
8. Spoon the mascarpone over the blueberries before serving!

Nutritional Information:

- **Calories:** 285
- **Fat:** 26 grams
- **Protein:** 5 grams
- **Total carbs:** 11 grams
- **Net carbs:** 8 grams

Mini mixed berry cheesecake muffins

These beautiful treats combine two classics: muffins and cheesecake. We have an almond-based muffin bottom with a berry cheesecake top. These are ideal as a sweet afternoon treat or even as an easy dessert.

Serves: 12
Time: approximately 35 minutes
Ingredients:

- 2 cups ground almonds
- 1 tsp Stevia/your preferred keto sweetener
- 1 ½ tsp baking powder
- 3 eggs
- ½ cup cream
- 1 tsp vanilla extract

Cheesecake topping:

- 9 oz full-fat, plain cream cheese
- 2 eggs
- 1 tsp Stevia/your preferred keto sweetener
- 1 ½ cups mixed berries (I use blueberries, strawberries and raspberries)

Method:

1. Preheat the oven to 360 degrees Fahrenheit and line a 12-hole muffin pan with cupcake cases
2. In a large bowl, beat together the cream cheese, eggs and stevia until thick, soft and combined, set aside as you prep the muffin batter
3. Combine the ground almonds, sweetener and baking powder in a large bowl
4. In a small bowl, whisk together the eggs, cream and vanilla extract until combined
5. Gently fold the wet ingredients into the dry ingredients until just combined
6. Spoon the batter into the prepared cupcake cases
7. Sprinkle *half* of the berries over the muffin batter
8. Spoon the cheesecake mixture over the muffin batter and berries and place the rest of the berries over the cheesecake mixture
9. Place the pan into the oven and bake until the cheesecake portion is set and the muffin batter is cooked through, (stick a skewer into the cupcakes and there should only be cheesecake on the skewer when you take it out)
10. Leave to cool before devouring!

Nutritional Information:

- **Calories:** 211
- **Fat:** 18 grams
- **Protein:** 7 grams
- **Total carbs:** 6 grams
- **Net carbs:** 4 grams

Vanilla custard

Vanilla custard is an essential dessert staple. Pour it over keto cakes or serve alone with a few fresh berries. It's important to use pure vanilla extract as opposed to vanilla essence.

Serves: 4

Time: approximately 20 minutes

Ingredients:

- 1 ½ cups heavy cream
- 1 Tbsp vanilla extract
- 3 egg yolks
- ½ tsp Stevia/your preferred keto sweetener

Method:

1. Place a heatproof bowl over a saucepan of simmering water
2. Place the cream, vanilla extract, egg yolks and sweetener into the bowl and whisk to combine
3. Keep whisking as the custard thickens, it may take a while, stick with it!
4. Pour the thickened custard into a jug and store in the fridge until needed

Nutritional Information:

- **Calories:** 364
- **Fat:** 37 grams
- **Protein:** 4 grams
- **Total carbs:** 4 grams
- **Net carbs:** 4 grams

Berry Coulis

Berry coulis is a tart, refreshing sauce made from frozen berries, sweetener and a little lemon juice. It's the perfect keto-friendly sauce for chocolate cake or keto ice cream. This is perfect for anyone who doesn't like chocolate sauce or who cannot eat dairy-based sauces. I love to make this sauce in the Summertime and drizzle it over anything...even over my yogurt in the morning! To increase the fat factor we add avocado oil, which actually helps to create a silkier texture.

Serves: 5
Time: approximately 15 minutes
Ingredients:

- ½ cup frozen strawberries
- ½ cup frozen raspberries
- ½ cup frozen blueberries
- 1 tsp Stevia/your preferred keto sweetener
- Juice of 1 lemon
- 3 Tbsp avocado oil

Method:

1. Place all ingredients into a food processor and blitz until very smooth
2. Transfer the coulis into a sieve and place it over a bowl
3. Use a spatula to press the coulis through the sieve and into the bowl below, this will leave the berry seeds in the sieve, and will create a super smooth coulis
4. Discard the seeds in the sieve and transfer the coulis to a pouring jug and store in the fridge until needed

Nutritional Information:

- **Calories:** 96
- **Fat:** 8 grams
- **Protein:** 0 grams
- **Total carbs:** 7 grams
- **Net carbs:** 5 grams

Lemon Curd

Lemon curd is like custards' delicious best friend. I love a very tart, tangy, zesty lemon curd so I add lots of fresh lemon juice to my recipe! Lemon curd has a multitude of uses; dolloped over keto ice cream, slathered onto keto cake, swirled into plain yogurt or eaten off the spoon for a quick treat.

Serves: 6

Time: approximately 25 minutes

Ingredients:

- 4 oz butter
- 1 tsp Stevia/your preferred keto sweetener
- Juice and zest of 5 lemons
- 3 whole eggs
- 2 egg yolks

Method:

1. Place a heatproof bowl over a saucepan of simmering water
2. Add the butter, sweetener, lemon zest and juice to the bowl and stir as the butter melts
3. Whisk as you add the eggs and egg yolks to the bowl and keep whisking as the curd thickens (it should be able to coat the back of a spoon)
4. Pour the curd into sterilized jars or pouring jugs and store in the fridge until needed

Nutritional Information:

- **Calories:** 198
- **Fat:** 19 grams
- **Protein:** 4 grams
- **Total carbs:** 4 grams
- **Net carbs:** 4 grams

Spiced stewed Rhubarb

Sometimes we just feel like a dessert which isn't necessarily creamy or chocolatey. We crave a fruity, tart and refreshing dessert which still has just a little hint of sweetness and buttery richness. Well, that's what this recipe gives us! Rhubarb is a fantastically nutritious food and it's totally fine "on keto" in small amounts. Spoon over yogurt, serve as a tart accompaniment to cakes or swirl into vanilla keto custard.

Serves: 4

Time: approximately 30 minutes

Ingredients:

- 3 cups chopped fresh rhubarb
- 1 tsp Stevia/your preferred keto sweetener
- 1 tsp vanilla extract
- Juice of ½ lemon
- 3 Tbsp butter
- 1 cup water

Method:

1. Place all ingredients into a large saucepan and place over a medium heat
2. Bring the mixture to boiling point then reduce to a simmer
3. Allow the mixture to simmer away until the rhubarb is nice and soft and the liquids have reduced
4. Store in an airtight jar in the fridge until required!

Nutritional Information:

- **Calories:** 100
- **Fat:** 9 grams
- **Protein:** 1 gram
- **Total carbs:** 3 grams
- **Net carbs:** 3 grams

Berry chia pudding

This recipe can be pulled out of the bag for dessert AND breakfast. Chia seeds are lovely little balls of fat and fiber, great for fueling your day. We hydrate the chia seeds with cream, almond milk and vanilla extract. We add berries and voila! Pudding/breakfast heaven.

Serves: makes 4 individual puddings

Time: approximately 10 minutes active prep time plus overnight in the fridge

Ingredients:

- 8 Tbsp black chia seeds
- 4 tsp vanilla extract
- 2 tsp Stevia/your preferred keto sweetener
- 1 ½ cups heavy cream
- 1 cup unsweetened almond milk
- 1 cup mixed berries (I use strawberries, raspberries and blueberries)

Method:

1. Combine all ingredients in a large bowl and leave for about 5 minutes to allow the mixture to start the thickening process as the chia seeds hydrate
2. Divide the mixture into four dessert dishes (or small bowls), cover and place into the fridge overnight
3. Give the pudding a stir before serving with a couple of extra fresh berries on top!

Nutritional Information:

- **Calories:** 469
- **Fat:** 40 grams
- **Protein:** 8 grams
- **Total carbs:** 11 grams
- **Net carbs:** 5 grams

Frozen Desserts

On a hot, balmy evening, there's nothing better than a cold dessert after a tasty keto dinner. This section is a carefully curated collection of frozen desserts from classics such as vanilla ice cream to unique treats such as peanut butter ice cream cupcakes. We've also got a few different variations of Froyo (I secretly like Froyo better than ice cream!). These desserts are really easy to make and are designed to be whipped up quickly and easily before being thrown in the freezer to firm up and become icy fresh!

Classic Vanilla Ice Cream

Vanilla ice cream will forever be a favorite dessert either on its own or as an accompaniment to cakes, pies and brownies. This recipe doesn't require an ice cream maker and it's really easy to whip up. We use coconut oil for a smooth texture and extra healthy fats!

Serves: 6

Time: approximately 20 minutes active prep time plus freezing overnight

Ingredients:

- 3 cups heavy cream
- 2 Tbsp butter
- 1 tsp Stevia/your preferred keto sweetener
- 3 tsp vanilla extract
- ½ cup coconut oil

Method:

1. Place TWO CUPS of cream into a saucepan with the butter, sweetener, vanilla and coconut oil, place over a medium heat
2. Allow the mixture to come to a simmer as you whisk. Remove from the heat and allow to cool
3. Beat the leftover one cup of cream until soft and thick
4. Fold the cooled cream/vanilla mixture into the whipped cream, being careful not to deflate the whipped cream too much
5. Pour the mixture into an ice cream container or plastic container, place the lid on top
6. Place the ice cream into the freezer and give it a stir every hour for the first five hours (if possible) to help the ice cream to become creamy and fluffy
7. Serve however you like!

Nutritional Information:

- **Calories:** 613
- **Fat:** 66 grams
- **Protein:** 2 grams
- **Total carbs:** 4 grams
- **Net carbs:** 4 grams

Lemon and Raspberry sorbet

Sorbet is like the dairy-free best friend of ice cream. It's tart, tangy, sweet and incredibly refreshing. I love it served simply on its own on a very hot Summer day or evening. This sorbet is super simple, made from raspberries, lemon juice and sweetener. No egg whites, sugars or ice cream churner required!

Serves: 6
Time: approximately 10 minutes prep time plus freezing overnight
Ingredients:

- 3 cups frozen raspberries
- Juice of 3 ripe lemons
- 1 tsp Stevia/your preferred keto sweetener
- 3 Tbsp coconut oil

Method:

1. Place all ingredients into a food processor and blend until completely smooth
2. Transfer the sorbet into an ice cream container or plastic container and smooth out the top
3. Place the lid on top and place the sorbet into the freezer. Give it a good stir every hour for the first five hours to help the texture to become creamy as opposed to icy
4. Serve with a lemon wedge and enjoy!

Nutritional Information:

- **Calories:** 97
- **Fat:** 7 grams
- **Protein:** 1 gram
- **Total carbs:** 9 grams
- **Net carbs:** 5 grams

Raspberry and almond Froyo

Froyo is a genius invention. As a lover of tangy foods, I LOVE froyo and often crave it even more than ice cream. This recipe uses bold, bright, tasty raspberries for a fresh, vibrant flavor. But that's not all...we fold toasted almonds into the mix for a crunchy, nutty addition.

Serves: 8

Time: approximately 10 minutes plus freezing overnight

Ingredients:

- 1 cup heavy cream
- 2 cups full-fat Greek yogurt
- 1 ½ cups frozen raspberries
- ¾ cup slivered almonds, toasted
- 1 tsp Stevia/your preferred keto sweetener

Method:

1. Whip the cream until it is soft, fluffy and thick but not buttery
2. Fold the yogurt, raspberries, almonds and sweetener into the cream until thoroughly combined
3. Transfer the yogurt mixture into an ice cream container or plastic container, place the lid on and pop it into the freezer
4. If you can, give the froyo a stir every hour for the first five hours. This will help the froyo to freeze into a thick, creamy, fluffy texture
5. Serve and enjoy!

Nutritional Information:

- **Calories:** 263
- **Fat:** 23 grams
- **Protein:** 6 grams
- **Total carbs:** 9 grams
- **Net carbs:** 7 grams

Peanut butter ice cream cupcakes

I was trying to think of a way to incorporate peanut butter into a frozen dessert without opting for a simple peanut butter ice cream. I took it a step further and thought, "why not make ice cream cupcakes?!!!". You simply fill cupcake cases with a creamy, peanut buttery ice cream filling and then top them with a cream cheese frosting. Before you serve the cupcakes, leave them out at room temperature for 10 minutes to soften slightly.

Serves: 8

Time: approximately 20 minutes prep time plus at least 5 hours of freezing time

Ingredients:

- 2 cups heavy cream
- 1 tsp Stevia/your preferred keto sweetener
- 4 Tbsp peanut butter (any kind, as long as it's natural and unsweetened)
- 3 egg yolks

Frosting:

- 5 oz plain, full-fat cream cheese
- ½ cup heavy cream
- ½ tsp Stevia/your preferred keto sweetener

Method:

1. Line 8 muffin holes in a muffin pan with cupcake cases and set aside
2. Place ONE CUP of the cream into a saucepan with the stevia and peanut butter, bring to a gentle simmer then take off the heat
3. Spoon a little of the hot cream mixture into the egg yolks and quickly whisk
4. Transfer the egg yolk mixture into the saucepan of cream mixture and place back onto a low heat, stirring as it thickens, set aside to cool
5. Whip the remaining one cup of cream until soft and fluffy
6. Fold the whipped cream into the cream/peanut butter mixture until combined
7. Spoon the mixture into the cupcake cases and put in the freezer as you make the frosting
8. To make the frosting: beat together the cream cheese, cream and sweetener until thick and smooth
9. Spoon the cream cheese mixture over the peanut butter cupcakes and pop back into the freezer
10. Eat the cupcakes when they're frozen but not totally hard (leaving them out for 10 minutes at room temperature helps)

Nutritional Information:

- **Calories:** 379
- **Fat:** 38 grams
- **Protein:** 5 grams
- **Total carbs:** 6 grams
- **Net carbs:** 5 grams

Blueberry almond ice cream pops

These ice cream pops are a little sophisticated, super pretty and really tasty. You will need a set of popsicle molds to make these. We use almond essence for a subtle hint of almond flavor, and toasted almonds for toasty, nutty flavor. Blueberries add color, sweetness and antioxidants.

Serves: 8

Time: approximately 15 minutes prep time plus overnight in the freezer

Ingredients:

- 3 cups heavy cream
- 3 egg yolks
- 1 ½ tsp Stevia/your preferred keto sweetener
- Few drops of almond essence
- ¾ cup chopped almonds, toasted
- 1 cup fresh blueberries

Method:

1. Place TWO CUPS of the cream, the egg yolks, sweetener and almond essence into a saucepan and whisk to combine
2. Place the saucepan over a medium heat and keep whisking as the mixture heats and begins to thicken
3. Take the saucepan off the heat and set aside to cool
4. Whip the remaining cup of cream until soft and fluffy
5. Gently stir together the cooled egg yolk/cream mixture and whipped cream
6. Fold the chopped almonds and blueberries into the mixture
7. Spoon the mixture into your popsicle molds and pop into the freezer to freeze overnight
8. Before serving, leave the popsicle molds out at room temperature for a few minutes before sliding the ice creams out and passing around to eager guests!

Nutritional Information:

- **Calories:** 314
- **Fat:** 31 grams
- **Protein:** 4 grams
- **Total carbs:** 6 grams
- **Net carbs:** 5 grams

Coffee cheesecake ice cream

This dessert is a combination of coffee, cheesecake and ice cream, all piled into one container. You will need instant espresso powder for this recipe, it's very important! Serve alone or with a shot of espresso, Affogato style.

Serves: 8

Time: approximately 15 minutes prep time plus overnight in the freezer

Ingredients:

- 2 cups heavy cream
- 1 ½ tsp Stevia/your preferred keto sweetener
- 4 tsp instant espresso powder
- 9 oz plain, full-fat cream cheese

Method:

1. Whip the cream, stevia and instant coffee powder until soft, fluffy and thick, set aside
2. Give the cream cheese a good, hard stir to soften it
3. Fold the whipped cream mixture into the stirred cream cheese until combined
4. Spoon the mixture into an ice cream container or plastic container, place the lid on top and pop it into the freezer
5. Give the ice cream a good stir every hour for the first five hours of freezing time. This will help to achieve a fluffy, creamy texture
6. Serve alone, with coffee or as an accompaniment to keto cake or brownie!

Nutritional Information:

- **Calories:** 281
- **Fat:** 29 grams
- **Protein:** 3 grams
- **Total carbs:** 3 grams
- **Net carbs:** 3 grams

Tangy lime and tequila popsicles

Let's switch gears toward a tangier, more grown-up direction. These popsicles are a little bit naughty...they've got tequila in them! It's kind of like a margarita in a popsicle. Obviously, these should only be served to people over 21 (or 18, depending on where you are!). These popsicles are a perfect way to start a Summertime party or keto cocktail hour!

Serves: 6

Time: approximately 10 minutes prep time plus overnight in the freezer

Ingredients:

- ½ cup fresh lime juice
- Juice of 2 lemons
- 1 tsp Stevia/your preferred keto sweetener
- 2 cups water
- 4 oz tequila

Method:

1. Place all ingredients into a saucepan and bring to a simmer, remove from the heat and allow to cool completely
2. Stir the tequila into the mixture
3. Pour the mixture into popsicle molds and place into the freezer to freeze overnight
4. If you don't have popsicle molds, you could pour the mixture into a container and turn it into sorbet as opposed to individual popsicles

Nutritional Information:

- **Calories:** 53
- **Fat:** 0 gram
- **Protein:** 0 gram
- **Total carbs:** 3 grams
- **Net carbs:** 2 grams

Frozen coconut blackberry whip

Here we have a fluffy, creamy, tropical-inspired dessert for all coconut lovers. We combine whipped cream with coconut cream, toasted coconut and sweet, jewel-toned blackberries. Serve alone, with keto chocolate sauce or on the side of keto cakes or brownies.

Serves: 10

Time: approximately 15 minutes prep time plus overnight in the freezer

Ingredients:

- 1 ½ cups heavy cream
- 1 ½ cups full fat coconut cream
- 1 cup unsweetened toasted dried coconut
- 1 ½ tsp Stevia/your preferred keto sweetener
- 1 ½ cups blackberries

Method:

1. Whip the cream until soft and fluffy
2. Whip the coconut cream until soft and fluffy (I find it easier to whip the cream and coconut cream separately)
3. Combine the whipped cream and coconut cream in a large bowl
4. Stir the toasted coconut, sweetener and blackberries into the whipped cream mixture
5. Spoon the mixture into an ice cream container or plastic container and place the lid on top
6. Place the container into the freezer and give it a vigorous stir every hour for the first five hours of freezing
7. Enjoy however you wish!

Nutritional Information:

- **Calories:** 284
- **Fat:** 26 grams
- **Protein:** 2 grams
- **Total carbs:** 7 grams
- **Net carbs:** 6 grams

Keto pistachio icebox cake

Icebox cakes have become super popular over the past couple of years, thanks to their simplicity and Instagram-worthy prettiness. This cake has a nutty base (to mimic Graham crackers) and a creamy, pistachio-flavored top. We add a drop or two of green food coloring to increase the green factor!

Serves: 10

Time: approximately 20 minutes prep time plus overnight in the freezer

Ingredients:

- 1 cup finely chopped almonds (not ground almonds)
- ½ cup ground hazelnuts
- 4 oz butter, melted
- 2 cups heavy cream
- 1 ½ tsp Stevia/your preferred keto sweetener
- 3 egg yolks
- 1 cup chopped pistachios
- Few drops of green food coloring (optional)

Method:

1. Grease a cake pan with butter and set aside
2. Combine the almonds, hazelnuts and melted butter in a bowl until they reach a wet sand consistency
3. Press the nut/butter mixture into the bottom of your prepared cake pan
4. Place ONE CUP of the cream, the sweetener and egg yolks into a saucepan and place over a medium heat
5. Whisk the cream/egg mixture as it heats and begins to thicken, remove from the heat and allow to cool
6. Whip the remaining cup of cream until thick and soft
7. Fold the whipped cream into the cooled cream/egg mixture until combined
8. Fold the pistachios and food coloring (if using) into the mixture and spoon into your nut-lined cake pan, smooth out the top
9. Cover the cake with plastic wrap and place into the freezer overnight
10. Slice and serve!

Nutritional Information:

- **Calories:** 406
- **Fat:** 41 grams
- **Protein:** 7 grams
- **Total carbs:** 8 grams
- **Net carbs:** 5 grams

Froyo Bark with Chocolate, macadamia nuts and strawberries

Last in this icy section of frozen goodies is a delicious "bark", which basically means delicious shards of tastiness. This particular bark is made from a yogurt base with chocolate (yum), macadamia nuts (crunch) and strawberries (sweet and Summery!).

Serves: 12

Time: approximately 10 minutes prep time plus overnight in the freezer

Ingredients:

- 2 cups full-fat Greek yogurt
- 1 tsp Stevia/your preferred keto sweetener
- 5 oz 72% cocoa dark chocolate, roughly chopped
- ¾ cup chopped roasted macadamia nuts
- 1 cup chopped strawberries

Method:

1. Line a high-rimmed baking tray with baking paper and set aside
2. Stir together the yogurt and stevia
3. Spread the yogurt onto your lined baking tray
4. Sprinkle the chocolate, macadamia nuts and strawberries over the yogurt
5. Pop the tray into the freezer (on an even surface) and freeze overnight
6. Break the frozen yogurt into uneven shards and devour!

Nutritional Information:

- **Calories:** 161
- **Fat:** 12 grams
- **Protein:** 4 grams
- **Total carbs:** 10 grams
- **Net carbs:** 5 grams

Dairy-Free Desserts

If you're lactose intolerant, vegan or simply choose to avoid dairy, then this section is especially for you! Also...sorry about all the creamy stuff in the rest of these recipes. Absolutely anyone can enjoy these recipes, as they're all incredibly delicious. We've got fruity mousse, nutty ice cream, tropical cupcakes, custard, fudge balls and more!

Dairy-free raspberry mousse

We're kicking things off with a bang! This mousse is tangy and sweet, thanks to the world's best berry, the raspberry. This recipe uses gelatin to reach that thick, "suspended in air" texture. Instead of cream we use coconut cream, which goes impeccably well with raspberries.

Serves: 5

Time: approximately 30 minutes prep time plus at least an hour in the fridge

Ingredients:

- 1 tsp gelatin
- ½ cup water
- 1 tsp Stevia/your preferred keto sweetener
- 2 cups full-fat coconut cream
- 1 tsp vanilla extract
- 1 ½ cups fresh raspberries

Method:

1. Place the water into a saucepan over a medium-high heat until it reaches a gentle simmer
2. Add the gelatin to the water and stir as it dissolves into the water. Take the pan off the heat and allow the gelatin mixture to cool
3. Place the coconut cream, sweetener and vanilla extract into a large bowl and whip with electric beaters until thick, soft and creamy
4. Keep beating as you pour the gelatin water into the whipped coconut cream until it's completely incorporated
5. Fold the raspberries into the mixture
6. Spoon the mousse into five glass dessert dishes
7. Place into the fridge for about an hour or until set
8. Serve and enjoy!

Nutritional Information:

- **Calories:** 253
- **Fat:** 24 grams
- **Protein:** 3 grams
- **Total carbs:** 8 grams
- **Net carbs:** 3 grams

Dairy-free lemon custard

What's halfway between custard and lemon curd? Lemon custard! This custard is made with almond milk and egg yolks, with a generous dose of fresh lemon juice and zest. I like to eat this custard alone...or dolloped onto keto cakes or bars.

Serves: 4

Time: approximately 30 minutes

Ingredients:

- 2 cups unsweetened almond milk
- 4 egg yolks
- 1 tsp Stevia/your preferred keto sweetener
- ½ cup fresh lemon juice
- Zest of 1 lemon
- ½ tsp cornstarch dissolved in 2 tsp water

Method:

1. Place all ingredients into a saucepan and whisk thoroughly to combine. Ensure the egg yolks are all totally incorporated into the liquids
2. Place the saucepan over a medium heat and keep stirring as the custard thickens. Don't leave the saucepan alone on the heat as you risk a burnt custard!
3. Pour the custard into a pouring jug or bottle and store in the fridge until required
4. Serve anyway you like!

Nutritional Information:

- **Calories:** 83
- **Fat:** 6 grams
- **Protein:** 4 grams
- **Total carbs:** 3 grams
- **Net carbs:** 2 grams

Dairy-free chocolate cookies

Cookie time! These cookies are so simple it's just silly. Once again, ground almonds come to our aid in the place of flour. Instead of butter we use coconut oil, and in place of chocolate? Well...we use chocolate, but most 72% dark chocolate varieties don't contain dairy.

Serves: 12

Time: approximately 25 minutes

Ingredients:

- 3 Tbsp coconut oil (melted, if your coconut oil has solidified)
- 1 egg
- 1 tsp vanilla extract
- ⅓ cup almond milk
- 1 tsp Stevia/your preferred keto sweetener
- 2 cups ground almonds
- 1 tsp baking powder
- 5 oz 72% cocoa dark chocolate, roughly chopped
- Pinch of salt

Method:

1. Preheat the oven to 360 degrees Fahrenheit and line a baking tray with baking paper
2. In a large bowl, whisk together the coconut oil, egg, vanilla extract, almond milk and stevia
3. Stir the ground almonds, baking powder, chocolate and salt into the wet ingredients until combined
4. Roll the mixture into balls and place them onto your prepared tray
5. Use a fork to gently press down the cookie balls
6. Place the tray into the oven and bake for about 15 minutes or until golden but still a little soft
7. Leave to cool before transferring to an airtight container to store

Nutritional Information:

- **Calories:** 198
- **Fat:** 17 grams
- **Protein:** 5 grams
- **Total carbs:** 7 grams
- **Net carbs:** 3 grams

Dairy-free coconut vanilla pie

There's something extremely satisfying about a fresh, full pie sitting in the fridge, waiting to be devoured. This particular pie is a coconut-vanilla pie with a nutty base and absolutely no dairy. A perfect dessert for the dairy-free keto dieters in your life (or just for you!).

Serves: 8

Time: approximately 15 minutes prep time plus 5 hours in the fridge, or overnight

Ingredients:
- 1 cup finely chopped toasted almonds
- ½ cup coconut flour
- ½ cup coconut oil
- 2 tsp gelatin
- ⅓ cup boiling water
- 2 cups full fat coconut cream
- 1 Tbsp vanilla extract
- 1 ½ tsp Stevia/your preferred keto sweetener

Method:
1. Grease a pie pan with coconut oil and set aside
2. Combine the chopped almonds, coconut flour and coconut oil until it resembles wet sand
3. Press the almond/coconut oil mixture into your prepared pie pan
4. Pour the boiling water over the gelatin in a small bowl and stir until the gelatin dissolves into the water, leave to cool
5. In a large bowl, whip the coconut cream, vanilla and sweetener until thick and fluffy
6. Stir the cold gelatin water into the coconut cream mixture and pour the mixture into the pie dish on top of your nutty base
7. Place the pie into the fridge to chill and set for at least five hours, or overnight
8. Slice, serve, enjoy!

Nutritional Information:
- **Calories:** 369
- **Fat:** 35 grams
- **Protein:** 5 grams
- **Total carbs:** 9 grams
- **Net carbs:** 4 grams

Dairy-free butterscotch fudge balls

What's yummier than chocolate? Butterscotch. Okay, well, maybe it's a tie. To create the classic butterscotch flavor, we use butterscotch essence which is found in most supermarkets. If you can't find butterscotch essence, simply use caramel essence. Salt is a key ingredient here, as butterscotch absolutely must be a lovely mixture of salty and sweet.

Serves: 12 (makes 12 balls, 1 ball per serving)
Time: approximately 10 minutes of prep time plus 1 hour in the fridge
Ingredients:

- 1 cup raw cashews
- ½ cup coconut cream
- 1 tsp Stevia/your preferred keto sweetener
- 1 ½ tsp sea salt
- 3 tsp butterscotch or caramel essence
- 2 Tbsp coconut oil
- 2 tsp vanilla extract
- 1 cup ground almonds

Method:

1. Line a baking tray with baking paper and set aside
2. Place the cashews, coconut cream, sweetener, sea salt, butterscotch, coconut oil and vanilla into a food processor and blitz until super smooth and creamy
3. Transfer the mixture into a bowl and stir in the ground almonds to create a thick, paste-like consistency
4. Roll the mixture into balls and place onto your prepared tray
5. Place the tray into the fridge to set and firm up for at least an hour
6. Store in an airtight container in the fridge!

Nutritional Information:

- **Calories:** 137
- **Fat:** 12 grams
- **Protein:** 3 grams
- **Total carbs:** 5 grams
- **Net carbs:** 4 grams

Dairy-free lemon drizzle cake

Lemon drizzle cake is one of my favorite desserts ever, so I had to share it with you. Of course, this particular version is keto-approved and dairy-free. The best part about this cake is the sticky, sour, citrusy lemon drizzle which we generously pour over the warm, out-of-the-oven cake. Serve with a dollop of coconut yogurt! A perfect afternoon tea treat.

Serves: 10

Time: approximately 50 minutes

Ingredients:
- 3 eggs, separated
- ½ cup fresh lemon juice
- Zest of 3 lemons
- ½ cup coconut oil
- 2 tsp Stevia/your preferred keto sweetener
- 1 tsp baking powder
- 2 cups ground almonds

Drizzle:
- ½ cup fresh lemon juice
- 1 tsp Stevia/your preferred keto sweetener

Method:
1. Preheat the oven to 360 degrees Fahrenheit and line a cake pan with baking paper
2. In a large bowl, beat the egg whites with electric egg beaters until very stiff
3. Whisk together the egg yolks, sweetener, lemon juice, lemon zest and coconut oil
4. Toss together the ground almonds and the baking powder
5. Take a little bit of your beaten egg whites and fold them into the egg/lemon mixture, then fold in a little bit of the ground almonds. Repeat this until all of the ingredients are combined. Be very gentle so you don't knock the air out of your egg whites! The air will help the cake to rise
6. Pour the batter into your prepared cake pan and pop it into your preheated oven to bake for about 30-40 minutes or until a skewer comes out clean
7. As the cake is baking, prepare the drizzle: place the lemon juice and sweetener into a saucepan with a dash of water and bring to a simmer. Simmer until the mixture is sticky and a little thicker than before
8. As soon as you take the cake out of the oven, pour the drizzle over the top and leave to soak in!
9. Serve warm, with a dollop of coconut yogurt

Nutritional Information:
- **Calories:** 236
- **Fat:** 22 grams
- **Protein:** 6 grams
- **Total carbs:** 6 grams
- **Net carbs:** 3 grams

Dairy-free coffee fudge mug cake

If you've got a mug and a microwave, you can make this mug cake! And you should, because it's delicious. It has a rich, deep mocha flavor provided by cocoa and espresso powder, with ground almonds and coconut milk to bind it all together.

Serves: 2 (2 mug cakes)

Time: approximately 10 minutes

Ingredients:

- ⅔ cup ground almonds
- 3 Tbsp unsweetened cocoa powder
- 1 tsp baking powder
- Pinch of salt
- 2 tsp espresso powder
- 6 Tbsp almond milk
- ½ tsp vanilla extract
- ½ tsp Stevia/your preferred keto sweetener

Method:

1. Combine all ingredients in a small bowl and divide the mixture between two mugs
2. Place the mugs into the microwave and cook on high for 1 minute
3. Check the brownies and if they're still completely liquid then put them back in for 30 second intervals until you reach the desired doneness. I like mine to be super gooey in the middle but cooked around the edges
4. Serve with coconut yogurt!

Nutritional Information:

- **Calories:** 217
- **Fat:** 18 grams
- **Protein:** 8 grams
- **Total carbs:** 13 grams
- **Net carbs:** 6 grams

Dairy-free frosted coconut lime cupcakes

A delicate, sweet and generously-frosted cupcake is a thing of real beauty, especially when it's garnished with coconut threads and lime zest. We frost these beauties with coconut cream piled high!

Serves: 12

Time: approximately 40 minutes

Ingredients:

- 2 cups ground almonds
- 1 cup unsweetened dried coconut (the finely-chopped kind, not thread)
- 1 tsp Stevia/your preferred keto sweetener
- 1 tsp baking powder
- 3 eggs
- Juice and zest of 5 limes
- ½ cup coconut oil

Frosting:

- 1 cup coconut cream
- ½ cup unsweetened coconut thread
- Juice and zest of 1 lime
- ½ tsp Stevia/your preferred keto sweetener

Method:

1. Preheat the oven to 360 degrees Fahrenheit and line a 12-hole muffin pan with cupcake cases
2. In a large bowl, toss together the ground almonds, coconut, sweetener and baking powder
3. In a smaller bowl, beat together the eggs, lime juice and coconut oil
4. Fold the wet ingredients into the dry ingredients
5. Spoon the mixture into your prepared cupcake cases and pop the tray into the oven to bake for about 25-35 minutes or until just cooked. A skewer should come out clean
6. Leave the cupcakes to cool completely
7. Make the frosting: beat together the coconut cream, lime juice and sweetener until thick and fluffy
8. Spread the frosting over the cupcakes then sprinkle the coconut thread and lime zest over the top
9. Enjoy with a hot cup of coffee!

Nutritional Information:

- **Calories:** 299
- **Fat:** 29 grams
- **Protein:** 6 grams
- **Total carbs:** 6 grams
- **Net carbs:** 3 grams

Dairy-free pistachio-mint ice cream

Ice cream by no means needs to be a total "dairy fest". This dairy-free ice cream celebrates two of the best green dessert ingredients ever...pistachios and fresh mint. We use a basis of almond milk and coconut cream (for thickness and creaminess). For extra fat we use avocado oil (and extra greenness too!).

Serves: 8

Time: approximately 10 minutes prep time plus overnight in the freezer

Ingredients:

- 2 cups full-fat coconut cream
- 3 cups unsweetened almond milk
- 1 ½ cup chopped pistachios
- ⅓ cup finely chopped fresh mint
- 1 tsp Stevia/your preferred keto sweetener
- 4 Tbsp avocado oil

Method:

1. Use electric beaters to whip the coconut cream until soft, fluffy and thick
2. Carefully fold the almond milk, pistachios, mint, sweetener and avocado oil into the whipped coconut cream (don't worry if the coconut cream deflates, there will still be air hiding in there!)
3. Carefully transfer the mixture into an ice cream container or plastic container, place the lid on and pop it into the freezer
4. Give the ice cream a good stir every hour for the first five hours of freezing time
5. Scoop, serve, enjoy!

Nutritional Information:

- **Calories:** 366
- **Fat:** 36 grams
- **Protein:** 7 grams
- **Total carbs:** 9 grams
- **Net carbs:** 6 grams

Cream Cheese, Mascarpone and Ricotta Desserts

While there are many recipes containing cream cheese, mascarpone and ricotta in this book, I wanted to create a section dedicated to the very best ones. These recipes are all defined by and centered around creamy, cheesy, rich, soft cheeses. We have cheesecakes, tiramisu, ricotta cake and even a trio of cream cheese frosting ideas! Always remember to buy full fat dairy products and stay well away from anything "diet", "low fat" or "fat free".

Baked vanilla Cheesecake

Kicking this creamy section off is a classic vanilla cheesecake. For the base, we are making keto cookies which we crush and combine with melted butter. The filling is just as it should be - creamy, slightly tangy, light and rich.

Serves: 12

Time: approximately 2 hours including baking the cookies for the base

Ingredients:

Cookies for the base:

- 5 oz butter, softened
- 2 eggs
- 1 tsp Stevia/your preferred keto sweetener
- 1 tsp baking powder
- 1 ½ cups ground almonds
- 1 cup finely chopped walnuts

To make the base:

- All of the cookies you baked!
- 4 oz melted butter

Cheesecake filling:

- 1 lb plain cream cheese
- 10 ½ oz full fat sour cream
- 3 eggs
- 1 Tbsp vanilla extract
- 1 tsp Stevia/your preferred keto sweetener

Method:

1. Bake the cookies: preheat the oven to 360 degrees Fahrenheit and line a baking tray with baking paper. Beat the butter until soft and creamy. Add the eggs to the butter and beat thoroughly. Stir the sweetener, baking powder, ground almonds and walnuts into the egg/butter mix. Roll the dough into balls, place onto the lined tray, press down with a fork and bake for 20 minutes or until golden. Leave to cool completely
2. Preheat the oven to 360 degrees Fahrenheit and line a cake pan with baking paper and set aside
3. Place the cooked and cooled cookies into a food processor with the melted butter and pulse until you achieve a wet, sandy consistency
4. Press the cookie/butter mix into your lined cake pan and set aside

5. Pop the cream cheese and sour cream into the food processor and blitz until smooth and creamy. Add the eggs, vanilla and sweetener and process until combined and smooth

6. Pour the cream cheese mixture into your cookie-lined cake pan and pop it into the oven to bake for about an hour or until the edges of the cheesecake are cooked but the middle is still a little gooey

7. Leave to cool completely before slicing and serving!

Nutritional Information:

- **Calories:** 476
- **Fat:** 47 grams
- **Protein:** 10 grams
- **Total carbs:** 6 grams
- **Net carbs:** 4 grams

Italian Ricotta Cake

Ricotta cake is like a lighter, more elegant version of cheesecake. Ricotta cheese is soft and creamy, with a mild flavor which lends itself so beautifully to cake. This cake is delicately flavored with lemon. Served with sweetened mascarpone cheese and lemon zest, this is the perfect keto dessert for guests.

Serves: 8

Time: approximately 1 hour

Ingredients:

- 2 oz butter, softened
- 1 tsp Stevia/your preferred keto sweetener
- 4 eggs
- 9 oz full fat ricotta
- Juice and zest of 1 lemon
- 1 ½ cups ground almonds
- 2 tsp baking powder
- Pinch of salt

Method:

1. Preheat the oven to 360 degrees Fahrenheit and line a baking tray with baking paper
2. Beat together the butter and sweetener until soft and creamy
3. Add the eggs to the butter and beat until combined and fluffy
4. Add the ricotta, lemon juice and zest to the bowl and beat until combined and creamy
5. Fold the ground almonds, baking powder and salt into the buttery mixture until just incorporated
6. Pour the batter into your prepared pan and bake for about 45 minutes or until the center of the cake is spongy and bounces back when very gently pressed
7. Leave to cool before slicing and serving!

Nutritional Information:

- **Calories:** 199
- **Fat:** 17 grams
- **Protein:** 8 grams
- **Total carbs:** 5 grams
- **Net carbs:** 3 grams

Keto Tiramisu

The combination of almond biscuits, mascarpone cheese, coffee and a scattering of cocoa powder is as good as it gets. This tiramisu is good enough to be served to a table full of guests, keto or not!

Serves: 8

Time: approximately 1 hour including cooking and cooling the biscuits

Ingredients:

Biscuits:

- 3 oz butter, melted
- 1 egg
- ¼ tsp almond essence
- 1 tsp vanilla extract
- 1 cup ground almonds
- ½ cup slivered almonds, toasted
- ½ tsp Stevia/your preferred keto sweetener
- 1 tsp baking powder
- ¼ cup very strong espresso mixed with a tiny pinch of Stevia/your preferred keto sweetener
- 1 lb mascarpone cheese
- 1 Tbsp Marsala wine
- 1 tsp Stevia/your preferred keto sweetener

To top the tiramisu:

- 1 cup heavy cream
- ½ tsp Stevia/your preferred keto sweetener
- 2 Tbsp unsweetened cocoa powder

Method:

1. Preheat the oven to 360 degrees Fahrenheit and line a tray with baking paper
2. Whisk together the melted butter, egg, almond essence and vanilla extract
3. Stir the ground almonds, slivered almonds, sweetener and baking powder into the wet ingredients until thoroughly combined
4. Roll the dough into balls, place onto the lined tray and press down with your hand or a fork. Place the tray into the oven and bake for about 20 minutes or until the cookies are golden. Leave the cookies to cool completely
5. Crush the cooled biscuits and scatter them into a rectangular dish, pour the coffee over top and leave it to soak in
6. Stir together the mascarpone, sweetener and Marsala wine
7. Spoon the mascarpone mixture over the coffee-soaked biscuits

8. Whip the cream with the sweetener until soft and fluffy, spoon over the mascarpone
9. Sift the cocoa over the cream before serving!

Nutritional Information:

- **Calories:** 452
- **Fat:** 45 grams
- **Protein:** 7 grams
- **Total carbs:** 8 grams
- **Net carbs:** 5 grams

Mini ginger Cheesecakes

Instead of one large cheesecake, we're making mini cheesecakes in cupcake cases! The base and filling are flavored with warming ginger to offset the sweet creaminess. These are easy and quick to make, and are super impressive for guests!

Serves: 12

Time: approximately 45 minutes

Ingredients:

Base:

- 1 ½ cups ground almonds
- ½ cup roughly chopped walnuts
- 4 oz melted butter
- 1 tsp ground ginger
- Pinch of salt
- ½ tsp Stevia/your preferred keto sweetener

Filling:

- 1 lb full fat cream cheese
- 9 oz full fat sour cream
- 3 eggs
- 2 tsp ground ginger
- 1 tsp Stevia/your preferred keto sweetener

Method:

1. Preheat the oven to 360 degrees Fahrenheit and line a 12-hole muffin pan with cupcake cases
2. Combine all of the base ingredients until you achieve a sandy texture
3. Press the base mixture into the bottom of each cupcake case and set aside
4. In a large bowl, beat together all of the filling ingredients until smooth and combined
5. Spoon the filling into the cupcake cases on top of the nutty base
6. Place the tray into the oven and bake for about 30-40 minutes or until the cheesecakes are just set but still a little soft in the middle
7. Leave the cheesecakes to cool completely before eating with a dollop of whipped cream!

Nutritional Information:

- **Calories:** 321
- **Fat:** 30 grams
- **Protein:** 8 grams
- **Total carbs:** 5 grams
- **Net carbs:** 3 grams

Salted Chocolate mascarpone whip

This recipe is kind of like a mousse, but creamier and richer. We combine mascarpone cheese with cocoa, sea salt and whipped cream to create a moreish, heavenly, whipped dessert everyone can enjoy. Pile it into dessert dishes and serve with a fresh raspberry and a mint leaf for style.

Serves: 4

Time: approximately 15 minutes plus an hour in the fridge

Ingredients:

- ¾ cup heavy cream
- 9 oz full fat mascarpone cheese
- 3 Tbsp unsweetened cocoa powder
- 2 tsp vanilla extract
- 1 tsp Stevia/your preferred keto sweetener
- ½ tsp sea salt

Method:

1. Whip the cream until soft and fluffy
2. Add the rest of the ingredients to the whipped cream and stir until combined and smooth
3. Spoon the whip into four dessert dishes and place into the fridge to chill for at least an hour
4. Serve with a little sprinkle of cocoa powder on top!

Nutritional Information:

- **Calories:** 467
- **Fat:** 48 grams
- **Protein:** 6 grams
- **Total carbs:** 6 grams
- **Net carbs:** 5 grams

Ricotta parfait cups

This recipe could be eaten as a super special breakfast as well as a refreshing dessert. We layer sweetened ricotta cheese with berries and toasted nuts, all topped off with whipped cream!

Serves: 5
Time: approximately 10 minutes plus an hour in the fridge
Ingredients:

- 13 oz full fat ricotta cheese
- 3 oz full fat mascarpone cheese
- ¾ tsp Stevia/you preferred keto sweetener
- 1 tsp vanilla extract
- 1 cup mixed berries (strawberries, blueberries and raspberries)
- ¼ cup chopped walnuts
- ¼ cup chopped almonds
- ¾ cup heavy cream

Method:

1. Stir together the ricotta, mascarpone, sweetener and vanilla until smooth and combined
2. Spoon half of the ricotta mixture into four dessert dishes
3. Scatter the berries over the ricotta mixture
4. Spoon the rest of the ricotta mixture over the berries and finish by scattering the toasted nuts over the top
5. Pop the parfaits into the fridge to chill for at least an hour
6. Serve!

Nutritional Information:

- **Calories:** 402
- **Fat:** 36 grams
- **Protein:** 12 grams
- **Total carbs:** 8 grams
- **Net carbs:** 7 grams

Cream cheese frosting 3 ways

Cream cheese frosting is a total Godsend, especially for keto dieters! It makes any cake, cupcake or bar so much more decadent and impressive. Here are three different cream cheese frosting flavors for you to try!

Serves: makes enough to frost one large cake or 12 cupcakes

Time: approximately 15 minutes (each flavor)

Ingredients:

Mint choc chip cream cheese frosting:

- 1 lb full fat cream cheese
- 6 oz butter softened
- 2 tsp Stevia/your preferred keto sweetener
- 4 oz 72% cocoa dark chocolate, finely chopped
- 1 tsp peppermint essence
- Couple of drops of green food coloring (optional)

Mocha cream cheese frosting:

- 1 lb full fat cream cheese
- 6 oz butter softened
- 2 tsp Stevia/your preferred keto sweetener
- 2 Tbsp unsweetened cocoa powder
- 2 tsp instant espresso powder dissolved in 3 tsp water

Lemon and raspberry cream cheese frosting:

- 1 lb full fat cream cheese
- 6 oz butter softened
- 2 tsp Stevia/your preferred keto sweetener
- ¾ cup raspberries
- Zest and juice of 1 lemon

Method:

1. Beat together the cream cheese, butter and sweetener until soft and super creamy
2. Stir in your chosen flavorings until combined
3. Store in the fridge until required!

Nutritional Information: Mint choc chip cream cheese frosting

- **Calories:** 291
- **Fat:** 28 grams
- **Protein:** 4 grams
- **Total carbs:** 4 grams
- **Net carbs:** 2 grams

Nutritional Information: Mocha cream cheese frosting

- **Calories:** 237
- **Fat:** 24 grams
- **Protein:** 3 grams
- **Total carbs:** 2 grams
- **Net carbs:** 2 grams

Nutritional Information: Lemon and raspberry cream cheese frosting

- **Calories:** 240
- **Fat:** 24 grams
- **Protein:** 3 grams
- **Total carbs:** 3 grams
- **Net carbs:** 2 grams

Butter pecan mascarpone and ricotta cream cups

This is an ultra easy dessert. We whip together mascarpone and ricotta cheese then stir through buttery pecans, vanilla and a touch of sweetener. You could use this as the filling for a keto pie with a nut base, or simply eat it alone, out of a dessert dish.

Serves: 6

Time: approximately 20 minutes

Ingredients:

- 9 oz full fat mascarpone cheese
- 5 oz full fat ricotta cheese
- ⅓ cup heavy cream
- 2 tsp vanilla extract
- 1 tsp Stevia/your preferred keto sweetener
- 3 oz butter
- 1 ½ cups pecan nuts
- Pinch of sea salt
- Pinch of Stevia/your preferred keto sweetener

Method:

1. Whip together the mascarpone, ricotta, cream, vanilla and sweetener until thick and fluffy
2. Place the butter into a frying pan over a medium-high heat and allow the butter to melt and become frothy
3. Add the pecan nuts and sweetener to the hot butter and stir as the nuts toast and become coated in butter. The nuts should be golden, fragrant and have a delicious toasted flavor when tasted
4. Leave the pecans to cool before folding them into the ricotta/mascarpone mixture
5. Spoon the mixture into dessert dishes and place into the fridge to chill for at least an hour before serving!

Nutritional Information:

- **Calories:** 580
- **Fat:** 60 grams
- **Protein:** 8 grams
- **Total carbs:** 6 grams
- **Net carbs:** 3 grams

Pistachio ricotta cakes with mascarpone frosting

We finish this section with sweet, lovely little cakes flavored with pistachio nuts. These cakes are made with ricotta cheese for a light, creamy texture and taste, with mascarpone dolloped on top. These little cakes are perfect for impressing keto guests for afternoon tea or dessert.

Serves: 12
Time: approximately 45 minutes

Ingredients:
- 2 cups ground almonds
- ¾ cup crushed pistachios
- 1 tsp baking powder
- 1 ½ tsp Stevia/your preferred keto sweetener
- 2 tsp vanilla extract
- 4 eggs
- 9 oz full fat ricotta cheese

Frosting:
- 9 oz full fat mascarpone
- ½ tsp Stevia/your preferred keto sweetener
- ½ cup crushed pistachios

Method:
1. Preheat the oven to 360 degrees Fahrenheit and grease a 12-hole muffin pan with butter
2. Stir together the ground almonds, pistachios, baking powder and sweetener
3. In a separate bowl, beat the vanilla, eggs and ricotta cheese until smooth
4. Fold the egg mixture into the dry ingredients until just combined
5. Spoon the batter into your prepared muffin pan and place it into the oven to bake for approximately 35 minutes or until the cakes bounce back when touched
6. Make the frosting: stir together the mascarpone, sweetener and pistachios
7. Leave the cakes to cool completely before slathering with frosting!

Nutritional Information:
- **Calories:** 308
- **Fat:** 27 grams
- **Protein:** 11 grams
- **Total carbs:** 8 grams
- **Net carbs:** 5 grams

Cakes, Cookies and Bars

Fill your home with the aroma of freshly baked goods. Home baking is one of life's most relaxing and satisfying activities. Just because we are on keto it doesn't mean we have to deprive ourselves of a leisurely baking session. This section is a carefully curated selection of cakes, cookies and bars for you to enjoy for dessert, morning tea, afternoon tea and any time when a sweet craving strikes.

Citrus cake with cream cheese frosting

We're starting this section with a citrus cake fit for any birthday, Sunday lunch or celebration which calls for an impressive and crowd-pleasing dessert. We use lemon, lime and orange zest to flavor the simple cake, with a citrusy cream cheese frosting.

Serves: 10

Time: approximately 1 hour

Ingredients:

- 2 cups ground almonds
- 1 tsp baking powder
- 1 tsp Stevia/your preferred keto sweetener
- 3 eggs
- 1 cup full fat sour cream
- ½ cup grapeseed oil (or any other flavorless/mild oil)
- Zest and juice of 1 lime
- Zest and juice of 1 lemon
- Zest and juice of 1 orange

Frosting:

- 9 oz full fat cream cheese
- 4 oz butter, softened
- 1 tsp Stevia/your preferred keto sweetener
- Zest of 1 lime
- Zest of 1 lemon
- Zest of 1 orange

Method:

1. Preheat the oven to 360 degrees Fahrenheit and line a cake pan with baking paper
2. In a large bowl, toss together the ground almonds, baking powder and sweetener
3. In a smaller bowl, whisk together the eggs, sour cream, oil, zest and juice of the lime, lemon and orange until combined and smooth
4. Pour the wet ingredients into the dry ingredients and stir together until combined and smooth
5. Pour the batter into your prepared cake pan and pop into your preheated oven to bake for about 40 minutes or until a skewer comes out clean
6. As the cake cools, make the frosting: beat together the cream cheese, butter, sweetener and all citrus zests until super smooth and fluffy
7. Leave the cake to cool completely before frosting with your citrus cream cheese frosting
8. Serve!

Nutritional Information:
- **Calories:** 453
- **Fat:** 44 grams
- **Protein:** 8 grams
- **Total carbs:** 8 grams
- **Net carbs:** 5 grams

Chocolate peppermint bars

Where I grew up, there were always chocolate peppermint bars in the cabinets at the best bakery in town. They are SO tasty I just had to recreate them for the keto diet. They have three layers, but they're really easy to make.

Serves: 16

Time: approximately 20 minutes plus 1 hour in the fridge to chill

Ingredients:

Base:

- 1 cup ground almonds
- 1 cup finely chopped walnuts
- 4 oz butter, melted
- 3 Tbsp unsweetened cocoa powder
- 1 tsp baking powder
- ½ tsp Stevia/your preferred keto sweetener

Filling:

- 2 cups unsweetened dried coconut (small pieces, not thread)
- 2 Tbsp butter, melted
- 2 Tbsp full fat cream
- 1 ½ tsp peppermint essence
- ½ tsp Stevia/your preferred keto sweetener

Topping:

- 8 oz 72% cocoa dark chocolate
- ½ cup heavy cream
- Pinch of salt

Method:

1. Preheat the oven to 360 degrees Fahrenheit and line a brownie pan with baking paper
2. Combine all of the base ingredients until fully combined and press the mixture into your prepared brownie pan
3. Pop the pan into the oven and bake the base for about 20 minutes, leave to cool completely
4. Stir together the filling ingredients until combined, and spread the mixture over your baked and cooled base and pop into the fridge as you make the topping
5. Make the topping: place the chocolate, cream and salt into a heatproof bowl over a saucepan of simmering water and stir as the chocolate melts into the cream, leave to cool slightly

6. Pour the melted chocolate mixture over the cooled filling and spread it out with a spatula
7. Place the pan into the fridge to chill before cutting into 16 bars

Nutritional Information:

- **Calories:** 296
- **Fat:** 28 grams
- **Protein:** 4 grams
- **Total carbs:** 8 grams
- **Net carbs:** 3 grams

Chocolate chip cookies

On a lazy weekend afternoon, one of the best ways to spend your time is by making a batch of chocolate chip cookies. These cookies are super low carb so you can enjoy a couple!

Serves: 20

Time: approximately 25 minutes

Ingredients:

- 2 tsp vanilla extract
- 5 oz butter, melted
- 2 eggs
- 2 cups ground almonds
- 1 ½ tsp Stevia/your preferred keto sweetener
- 6 oz 72% cocoa dark chocolate, roughly chopped
- 2 tsp baking powder
- Pinch of salt

Method:

1. Preheat the oven to 360 degrees Fahrenheit and line a baking tray with baking paper
2. In a large bowl, whisk together the vanilla, melted butter and eggs
3. Stir the ground almonds, sweetener, chocolate, baking powder and salt into the egg/butter mixture until thoroughly combined
4. Roll the dough into 20 balls and place them onto your prepared tray
5. Use a fork to press down the cookie dough balls and place the tray into the oven to bake for about 15 minutes or until the cookies are just turning golden but still soft
6. Leave the cookies to cool before eating or storing away in an airtight container

Nutritional Information:

- **Calories:** 163
- **Fat:** 15 grams
- **Protein:** 3 grams
- **Total carbs:** 4 grams
- **Net carbs:** 2 grams

Carrot cake with cream cheese frosting

It would be silly not to include carrot cake, considering it's an absolutely delicious classic. Carrot actually isn't a keto-friendly ingredient, but it's totally fine to use a small portion in a recipe which is split many ways. The spices are really important for that warming flavor. We finish the cake off with a generous pile of cream cheese frosting.

Serves: 10

Time: approximately 40 minutes

Ingredients:

- 2 cups ground almonds
- 2 tsp baking powder
- 1 tsp ground cinnamon
- ½ tsp ground allspice
- Pinch of salt
- 1 tsp Stevia/your preferred keto sweetener
- 4 eggs
- ½ cup flaxseed oil
- ¾ cup grated carrot
- 2 tsp vanilla extract

Frosting:

- 13 oz full fat cream cheese
- 4 oz butter, softened
- 1 tsp Stevia/your preferred keto sweetener
- ½ cup chopped walnuts

Method:

1. Preheat the oven to 360 degrees Fahrenheit and line a cake pan with baking paper
2. Toss together the ground almonds, baking powder, cinnamon, allspice, salt and sweetener in a large bowl
3. In a smaller bowl, whisk together the eggs, oil, carrot and vanilla
4. Pour the wet ingredients into the dry ingredients and stir to combine
5. Pour the batter into your prepared cake pan and place it into the preheated oven to bake for about 25 minutes or until the center bounces back when gently pressed
6. Leave the cake to cool completely before frosting with cream cheese frosting
7. To make the cream cheese frosting: beat together the cream cheese, butter and sweetener until thick and creamy. Spread the frosting over the cooled cake
8. Sprinkle the chopped walnuts over the frosted cake
9. Slice and serve!

Nutritional Information:

- **Calories:** 439
- **Fat:** 40 grams
- **Protein:** 13 grams
- **Total carbs:** 10 grams
- **Net carbs:** 7 grams

Hazelnut, coconut and orange cookies

This is the recipe to use when you're craving a cookie with a more sophisticated flavor profile. These cookies are made from hazelnuts and dried coconut and gently flavored with orange juice and zest.

Serves: 16

Time: approximately 30 minutes

Ingredients:

- 1 cup ground almonds
- 2 cups unsweetened coconut thread
- 1 cup chopped hazelnuts
- 1 tsp Stevia/your preferred keto sweetener
- Pinch of salt
- 1 tsp baking powder
- 4 oz butter, melted
- 2 eggs
- Juice and zest of 1 orange

Method:

1. Preheat the oven to 360 degrees Fahrenheit and line a baking tray with baking paper
2. Combine the ground almonds, coconut thread, hazelnuts, sweetener, salt and baking powder in a large bowl
3. In a separate bowl, whisk together the melted butter, eggs, orange juice and zest
4. Pour the wet ingredients into the dry ingredients and stir to combine
5. Place dollops of batter onto your prepared baking tray. Don't worry if the batter dollops look a little messy, they're meant to be!
6. Place the tray into the preheated oven and bake for about 20 minutes or until the cookies are golden brown
7. Leave the cookies to cool completely before eating!

Nutritional Information:

- **Calories:** 192
- **Fat:** 19 grams
- **Protein:** 4 grams
- **Total carbs:** 5 grams
- **Net carbs:** 3 grams

Vanilla birthday cake with thick vanilla frosting

No matter how old we get, there's something so exciting about a white birthday cake with white frosting, both flavored simply with vanilla. This cake is the keto answer to the classic vanilla birthday cake!

Serves: 12
Time: approximately 50 minutes
Ingredients:

- 3 cups ground almonds
- ½ cup ground hazelnuts
- 2 tsp baking powder
- Pinch of salt
- 1 ½ tsp Stevia/your preferred keto sweetener
- 2 Tbsp vanilla extract
- 1 cup full fat sour cream
- 4 eggs

Frosting:

- 5 oz butter, softened
- 1 lb full fat cream cheese
- 1 tsp Stevia/your preferred keto sweetener
- 2 Tbsp vanilla extract

Method:

1. Preheat the oven to 360 degrees Fahrenheit and line a cake pan with baking paper
2. Combine the ground almonds, ground hazelnuts, baking powder, sweetener and salt in a large bowl
3. In a separate bowl, whisk together the vanilla, sour cream and eggs until combined
4. Pour the wet ingredients into the dry ingredients and stir to combine
5. Pour the batter into your prepared cake pan and place it into the oven for about 30 minutes or until the cake is lightly golden on top and bounces back when you gently press it
6. Leave the cake to cool completely before frosting
7. Make the frosting as the cake cools: beat together the butter, cream cheese, sweetener and vanilla extract until smooth and creamy
8. Slice the cake in half (so you have a top and a bottom like a sandwich)
9. Spread 1 third of the frosting onto the bottom half of the cake then place the top half of the cake on top. Spread the remaining 2 thirds of the frosting over the cake and down the sides
10. Slice, serve and enjoy!

Nutritional Information:
- **Calories:** 452
- **Fat:** 39 grams
- **Protein:** 11 grams
- **Total carbs:** 8 grams
- **Net carbs:** 5 grams

Gooey lemon/lime bars

Lemon bars are a favorite in many people's households. I think it's partly because of the tangy flavor and partly because of the sticky, gooey texture. These bars take it one step further by using both lemons and limes.

Serves: 12

Time: approximately 40 minutes

Ingredients:

Base:

- 1 cup ground almonds
- ½ cup coconut flour
- 1 tsp Stevia/your preferred keto sweetener
- 3 oz butter, melted
- 1 egg
- 1 pinch salt
- 1 tsp baking powder

Filling:

- Juice and zest of 3 lemons
- Juice and zest of 3 limes
- 4 eggs
- 2 tsp cornstarch dissolved in 2 Tbsp water
- 1 tsp Stevia/your preferred keto sweetener

Method:

1. Preheat the oven to 360 degrees Fahrenheit and line a brownie pan with baking paper
2. Place all of the base ingredients into a food processor and pulse until everything comes together to form a wet, sand-like consistency
3. Press the base into the prepared pan and place into the oven to bake for 10 minutes while you prep the filling
4. Place all of the filling ingredients into the food processor (don't worry about cleaning it after making the base) and blitz until super smooth
5. Pour the filling into the pre-baked base and pop it back into the oven for about 15 minutes or until just set but still a little soft and gooey
6. Leave to cool completely before slicing into bars

Nutritional Information:

- **Calories:** 156
- **Fat:** 12 grams
- **Protein:** 5 grams
- **Total carbs:** 8 grams
- **Net carbs:** 4 grams

Walnut coffee bars

I adore the combination of coffee and walnut, especially when they're put together in a buttery, crumbly keto bar. Serve with super hot, strong coffee, a magazine and a leisurely hour to spare.

Serves: 12
Time: approximately 45 minutes
Ingredients:

- 1 cup ground almonds
- 1 cup finely chopped walnuts
- ½ cup ground linseed
- 1 tsp baking powder
- 2 tsp espresso powder dissolved in 1 Tbsp hot water
- 1 tsp Stevia/your preferred keto sweetener
- 2 eggs
- 5 oz butter, melted

Crumble top:

- 5 oz butter, cold
- 1 cup chopped walnuts
- 1 cup unsweetened coconut thread
- 1 tsp espresso powder
- ½ tsp Stevia/your preferred keto sweetener

Method:

1. Preheat the oven to 360 degrees Fahrenheit and line a brownie pan with baking paper or grease it thoroughly with butter
2. Combine the ground almonds, walnuts, linseed and baking powder in a large bowl
3. In a separate bowl, whisk together the dissolved espresso, stevia, eggs and butter
4. Pour the wet ingredients into the dry ingredients and stir to thoroughly combine
5. Press the mixture into your prepared pan and set aside as you make the crumble topping
6. Make the crumble topping: using a knife, chop the cooled butter into the walnuts, coconut thread, espresso powder and sweetener until you have a crumbly texture
7. Sprinkle the crumble over top of the base and pop the pan into the oven to bake for about 30 minutes or until golden
8. Leave to cool before slicing and serving!

Nutritional Information:

- **Calories:** 422
- **Fat:** 43 grams
- **Protein:** 8 grams
- **Total carbs:** 6 grams
- **Net carbs:** 2 grams

Chocolate fudge sandwich cookies

The only thing better than a chocolate cookie is TWO chocolate cookies, sandwiched together with chocolate mascarpone filling. While these are super impressive and will charm anyone who eats them, they're also very easy to whip up.

Serves: 10 sandwiches
Time: approximately 40 minutes

Ingredients:

- 3 oz 72% cocoa dark chocolate
- 5 oz butter, melted
- 2 eggs
- 3 Tbsp unsweetened cocoa powder
- 1 tsp Stevia/your chosen keto sweetener
- ½ tsp sea salt
- 1 tsp baking powder
- 2 cups ground almonds
- ⅓ cup coconut flour

Filling:

- 7 oz full fat mascarpone cheese
- ½ tsp Stevia/your chosen keto sweetener
- 1 Tbsp unsweetened cocoa powder

Method:

1. Preheat the oven to 360 degrees Fahrenheit and line a baking tray with baking paper
2. Place the chocolate and butter into a heatproof bowl over a saucepan of simmering water. Stir as the butter and chocolate melt together, remove from the heat and allow to cool
3. Whisk the eggs, cocoa, stevia and salt into the chocolate mixture
4. Stir the baking powder, ground almonds and cocoa powder into the chocolate/egg mixture until combined
5. Roll the mixture into 20 balls and place them onto your prepared baking tray. Use a fork to press the balls down
6. Pop the tray into the oven and bake for about 15 minutes or until the cookies are just set (they'll still be soft but they'll firm up a little more as they cool)
7. Leave the cookies to cool and make the filling as you wait: simply stir together the mascarpone, sweetener and cocoa powder

8. Spoon a generous dollop of mascarpone filling onto 10 of the cooled cookies and press the other 10 cookies on top so you have 10 sandwich cookies
9. Serve on a platter with a side of hot coffee!

Nutritional Information:

- **Calories:** 388
- **Fat:** 36 grams
- **Protein:** 8 grams
- **Total carbs:** 10 grams
- **Net carbs:** 4 grams

Truffles, Bombs and Balls

If you've been a keto dieter for a while, you'll know that "bombs" are a very popular keto snack. "Fat bombs" to be specific. I've extended this idea to truffles and balls! The difference is not completely defined, but I can tell you with complete confidence that they are all 100% delicious. These tasty truffles, bombs and balls are so easy to make and even easier to eat. Serve them as a light keto dessert for guests, eat as an after dinner treat or simply nibble on one during an afternoon slump. We've got fruity balls, peanut buttery bombs, chocolate truffles and many more...

Raspberry cheesecake balls

We're starting this delectable section with cheesecake in BALL FORM! I mean, how cute does it get?! As if that weren't enough, we add raspberries to complete this stunning collection of flavors. Not only are these balls delicious but they look super pretty and adorable too. We roll the balls in butter-toasted chopped almonds to represent the traditional Graham cracker cheesecake base.

Serves: 12 (12 balls, 1 ball per serving)

Time: approximately 15 minutes prep time plus an hour in the fridge

Ingredients:

- 1 cup chopped almonds
- 3 Tbsp butter
- 13 oz full fat cream cheese
- ½ cup ground almonds
- 1 tsp Stevia/your preferred keto sweetener
- 1 cup fresh raspberries
- 1 tsp vanilla extract

Method:

1. Line a baking tray with baking paper and set aside
2. Place the butter into a frying pan and place over a medium-high heat and allow the butter to melt
3. Once the butter has melted, add the chopped almonds to the butter and stir as the almonds toast and become golden brown and fragrant. Take off the heat and set aside
4. In a large bowl, combine the cream cheese, ground almonds, sweetener, raspberries and vanilla extract. Don't worry if the raspberries become mashed up in the cream cheese (they will!)
5. Spread the buttery toasted almonds onto a plate
6. Roll the cream cheese mixture into balls (yes, it will be very sticky but just roll with it!)
7. Roll the balls in the buttery almonds until they're totally coated
8. Place the coated cheesecake balls onto your prepared tray and pop into the fridge to chill and set for an hour or so
9. Store the balls in an airtight container in the fridge

Nutritional Information:

- **Calories:** 177
- **Fat:** 16 grams
- **Protein:** 4 grams
- **Total carbs:** 5 grams
- **Net carbs:** 3 grams

Peanut butter fat bombs

Peanut butter fat bombs really are a keto classic. These fat bombs are made with peanut butter (clearly!), cream cheese, coconut oil, vanilla and ground almonds. We use a little hit of sweetener to balance the saltiness of the peanut butter.

Serves: 18 (makes 18 bombs, 1 bomb per serving)

Time: approximately 15 minutes prep time plus 1 hour in the fridge

Ingredients:

- 1 cup peanut butter (any kind, as long as it's natural and unsweetened)
- 7 oz plain cream cheese
- 3 Tbsp coconut oil
- 1 tsp Stevia/your preferred keto sweetener
- 1 tsp vanilla extract
- ¾ cup ground almonds
- Little pinch of salt

Method:

1. Line a baking tray with baking paper
2. In a large bowl, mix together all ingredients until thoroughly combined. The mixture might be a little tough to stir at the start, but persevere and it will soften and become easier to combine
3. Roll the mixture into 18 balls and place them onto your prepared tray (like most of these ball/bomb/truffle recipes, this is sticky work!)
4. Place the tray into the fridge for about an hour to allow the bombs to chill and set
5. Store in an airtight container in the fridge

Nutritional Information:

- **Calories:** 159
- **Fat:** 14 grams
- **Protein:** 5 grams
- **Total carbs:** 5 grams
- **Net carbs:** 4 grams

Chocolate vanilla truffles

Finally we get to the chocolate! These truffles are pretty classic and not too out-of-the-box (why mess with something perfect?). However, they're completely elegant and delicious. Chocolate, vanilla, velvety smoothness...perfection.

Serves: 20 (makes 20 balls, 1 ball per serving)

Time: approximately 15 minutes prep time plus 1 hour in the fridge

Ingredients:

- 7 oz 72% cocoa dark chocolate
- 1 cup heavy cream
- 1 Tbsp vanilla extract
- ½ tsp Stevia/your preferred keto sweetener
- ½ cup unsweetened cocoa powder (for rolling)

Method:

1. Place the chocolate and cream into a heatproof bowl and place over a saucepan of boiling water
2. Stir as the chocolate melts into the cream
3. Stir the vanilla and sweetener into the chocolate/cream mixture and leave to cool completely
4. Spread the cocoa powder into the bottom of a shallow bowl
5. Use a metal dessert spoon to scoop small portions of chocolate mixture, very quickly roll the mixture into rough balls (they can be raggedy, truffles aren't meant to be totally round and smooth!)
6. Roll the balls in the cocoa powder until they're completely coated
7. Place the balls onto a plate and pop into the fridge to harden for an hour before serving or packing into an airtight container

Nutritional Information:

- **Calories:** 103
- **Fat:** 8 grams
- **Protein:** 1 gram
- **Total carbs:** 7 grams
- **Net carbs:** 6 grams

Salted chocolate and hazelnut balls

Chocolate, hazelnuts and salt are a fabulous trio. These balls are excellent as a mid-afternoon energy booster thanks to the high-energy ingredients such as butter and nuts.

Serves: 15

Time: approximately 10 minutes prep time plus 1 hour in the fridge

Ingredients:

- 5 oz butter, melted
- ½ cup ground almonds
- 1 cup finely chopped toasted hazelnuts
- 4 oz full fat ricotta cheese
- 1 tsp sea salt
- ½ tsp Stevia/your preferred keto sweetener
- 3 Tbsp unsweetened cocoa powder

Method:

1. Line a baking tray with baking paper
2. Combine all ingredients in a large bowl until completely combined
3. Roll the mixture into balls and place into your lined tray
4. Place the tray into the fridge for an hour to allow the balls to set and harden
5. Store the balls in an airtight container in the fridge until needed

Nutritional Information:

- **Calories:** 152
- **Fat:** 15 grams
- **Protein:** 3 grams
- **Total carbs:** 3 grams
- **Net carbs:** 1 gram

Coconut truffles

Anyone who loves all things coconut will go mad for these truffles. In reality, they're actually very similar to coconut macaroons (yup, macaROON, not to be confused with macaron). We combine toasted coconut with keto sweetener and egg whites. We then cook them in the oven until they become chewy and gooey.

Serves: 12 (makes 12 truffles, 1 truffle per serving)

Time: approximately 30 minutes

Ingredients:

- 2 cups unsweetened coconut thread
- 1 tsp Stevia/your prepared keto sweetener
- 3 egg whites, lightly beaten
- 2 Tbsp coconut flour
- 1 tsp vanilla extract

Method:

1. Preheat the oven to 350 degrees Fahrenheit and line a baking tray with baking paper
2. Heat a frying pan over a medium heat, do not add any oil to the pan, (it should be dry)
3. Add the coconut thread to the hot pan and stir as it toasts and becomes golden, take off the heat
4. Combine all ingredients in a large bowl
5. Roll the mixture into rough balls and place them onto your prepared tray
6. Place the tray into the oven and bake for about 15 minutes or until the truffles are golden
7. Leave the truffles to cool completely before storing them away in an airtight container

Nutritional Information:

- **Calories:** 85
- **Fat:** 7 grams
- **Protein:** 2 grams
- **Total carbs:** 4 grams
- **Net carbs:** 2 grams

Mocha truffles

If you need a chocolate hit as well as a caffeine shot, I've got just the thing for you. A lovely little ball of cocoa, coffee, almonds, ricotta and cream. These are the ideal truffles to serve to keto dieters after a keto meal. You could store these in the freezer to have as an emergency treat stash!

Serves: 15 (makes 15 balls, 1 ball per serving)

Time: approximately 10 minutes of prep plus 1 hour in the fridge

Ingredients:

- 1 cup ground almonds
- 4 Tbsp unsweetened cocoa powder
- 1 tsp Stevia/your preferred keto sweetener
- 3 Tbsp instant espresso powder, dissolved in 2 Tbsp hot water
- 1 cup heavy cream
- 7 oz full fat ricotta cheese

Method:

1. Line a baking tray with baking paper
2. In a large bowl, thoroughly combine all of the ingredients
3. Roll the mixture into 15 balls and place them onto the lined tray
4. Pop the tray into the fridge to cool and set the truffles for 1 hour
5. Store the truffles in an airtight container in the fridge
6. Serve with a hot coffee!

Nutritional Information:

- **Calories:** 124
- **Fat:** 12 grams
- **Protein:** 3 grams
- **Total carbs:** 3 grams
- **Net carbs:** 2 grams

Lemon fat bombs

These lemon bombs are like little explosions of citrusy sunshine. Because we use cream cheese as the basis, they have a very "cheesecake-y" vibe to them...which is a-okay with me. For extra fat, we add flaxseed oil. Tip: Flaxseed oil is fantastic for your skin!

Serves: 15 (makes 15 balls, 1 ball per serving)

Time: approximately 10 minutes of prep time plus 1 hour in the fridge

Ingredients:

- 9 oz full fat cream cheese
- 4 oz full fat ricotta cheese
- 3 Tbsp flaxseed oil
- ½ cup fresh lemon juice
- Zest of 2 lemons
- ¾ cup coconut flour
- 1 tsp Stevia/your preferred keto sweetener

Method:

1. Line a baking tray with baking paper
2. Combine all ingredients until fully incorporated
3. Roll the mixture into 15 balls and place them onto your lined tray
4. Pop the tray into the fridge for an hour so the balls can set and firm up
5. Store the bombs in an airtight container in the fridge

Nutritional Information:

- **Calories:** 102
- **Fat:** 8 grams
- **Protein:** 3 grams
- **Total carbs:** 4 grams
- **Net carbs:** 2 grams

Walnut brownie balls

What can I say? These are keto brownies in ball form! They're rolled in chopped toasted walnuts. We add sea salt to enhance the chocolate flavor, and a tiny hint of espresso powder for depth.

Serves: 15 (makes 15 balls, 1 ball per serving)

Time: approximately 15 minutes prep time plus 1 hour in the fridge

Ingredients:

- 4 oz 72% cocoa dark chocolate
- 3 Tbsp unsweetened cocoa powder
- 1 cup ground almonds
- 1 cup heavy cream
- 1 tsp Stevia/your preferred keto sweetener
- 1 tsp sea salt
- 1 tsp espresso powder
- 1 cup chopped toasted walnuts

Method:

1. Place the chocolate into a heatproof bowl over a saucepan of boiling water and stir as it melts, take off the heat and leave to cool
2. Stir together the melted chocolate, cocoa, almonds, cream, sweetener, sea salt, and espresso until completely combined
3. Spread the walnuts onto a plate
4. Roll the chocolate mixture into 15 balls and roll them in the walnuts until the balls are totally coated in walnuts
5. Pop the nut-coated balls onto a plate and allow them to chill in the fridge for at least an hour (you don't need to put them on a paper-lined tray because the nuts will prevent them from sticking)
6. Store the balls in an airtight container in the fridge

Nutritional Information:

- **Calories:** 205
- **Fat:** 19 grams
- **Protein:** 5 grams
- **Total carbs:** 7 grams
- **Net carbs:** 5 grams

Conclusion

It gives me great joy to think that you are embracing desserts while on the ketogenic diet...with the help of this book!

Take your time while creating your desserts and use it as an opportunity to relax and hang out with loved ones. Always remember to taste your desserts along the way to ensure you hit the right level of sweetness for your taste. It takes a little bit of experimentation when using different keto sweeteners, but that's part of the fun!

Never feel guilty about enjoying a delicious dessert when on keto. After all, as long as it fits your macro guidelines, it's completely guilt-free. Plus, dessert is the key to a sustained and successful keto diet...it helps to prevent any feelings of deprivation!

Have fun and happy dessert nibbling!

Made in the USA
Coppell, TX
06 November 2019